遊神與玄思

WANDERING MIND AND METAPHYSICAL THOUGHTS

遊神與玄思

Wandering Mind and Metaphysical Thoughts

高行健 著

Gao Xingjian

方梓勳 英譯

Translated by Gilbert C. F. Fong

中英雙語版

Chinese-English Bilingual Edition

The Chinese University Press

《遊神與玄思》
高行健 著
方梓勳 英譯

國際統一書號 : 978-962-996-838-0

出版：
中文大學出版社
香港中文大學 香港 新界 沙田
傳真：+852 2603 7355
電郵地址：cup@cuhk.edu.hk
網址：www.chineseupress.com

Wandering Mind and Metaphysical Thoughts
By Gao Xingjian
Translated by Gilbert C. F. Fong

ISBN: 978-962-996-838-0

Published by:
The Chinese University Press
The Chinese University of Hong Kong
Sha Tin, N.T., Hong Kong
Fax: +852 2603 7355
Email: cup@cuhk.edu.hk
Website: www.chineseupress.com

Printed in Hong Kong

目錄 Contents

鳴謝

譯者翻譯本書期間，幸蒙高行健博士耐心等候，不吝賜教，更慷允本書使用他的畫作和電影《美的葬禮》劇照為插圖，令本書生色不少，譯者不勝銘感。本書又得馮永莉女士仔細校對，尤其戴毅廷博士悉心審稿，一絲不苟，譯者亦一併致謝。

方梓勳

Acknowledgement

The translator would like to thank Dr. Gao Xingjian for his patience and guidance in the process of translating this collection, and for allowing the use of his paintings and stills from his movie *Requiem for Beauty* to adorn the pages of the book. My gratitude is also extended to Ms. Pamela Fung for proofreading, and especially to Dr. Eystein Thanisch for his tireless and meticulous effort in copyediting the poems.

Gilbert C. F. Fong

Gao

《妙不可言》 *Wonder*
1999, 47.5cm x 46cm.

前言 *

這是我第一本詩集，雖然從童年起就不斷寫詩，卻極少發表。記得是一九九一年，我已在巴黎定居，應臺灣的一些詩人朋友約稿，先後在《中國時報》和《現代詩》發表過幾篇。迄今已整整二十年，這次也是在老友林載爵先生的關心和催促下才整理出這本詩集。

我不自認為詩人，儘管詩歌可以說幾乎貫串我的創作，從專為舞蹈寫的劇目《聲聲慢變奏》到劇作《周末四重奏》和歌劇《八月雪》，乃至最近的電影詩《美的葬禮》，其文本都是詩篇。

---

* 本文原載《遊神與玄思》(台北：聯經出版社，2012)，本作〈後記〉，經作者同意改為本書的〈前言〉。

Preface*

This is my first book of poems. I have written poems since childhood, but few have been published. I remember that, in 1991 (at that time I was already living in Paris), several poets from Taiwan who were friends of mine asked me to write something for them. Subsequently, I published a few poems in *The China Times* and *Modern Poetry*. That was twenty years ago. Now, upon the urging of my good friend, Mr. Linden Tsai-Chueh Lin, the famous Taiwan publisher, I have finally managed to edit this collection of poems for publication under his care.

I do not consider myself a poet, although one could say that poetry runs through almost all my creative works, from the dance drama *Variations on a Slow Slow Tune* to the play, *Weekend Quartet*, and the opera, *Snow in August*. In my recent poetic film, *Requiem for Beauty*, the script is also composed of poems.

---

* The Preface, originally written as the Postscript to Gao Xingjian's *Youshen yu xuansi* 遊神與玄思 (*Wandering Mind and Metaphysical Thoughts*) (Taipei: Linking Books, 2012), is reproduced here with his permission.

這本詩集中收錄的五篇主要作品，其一〈我說刺蝟〉，不如說是一首戲作，我稱之為現代歌謠，也因為民間歌謠現時代已經被流行歌曲取代了。其二〈逍遙如鳥〉，原本是為電影寫的，我把我做的這種擺脱敘事結構的電影稱為電影詩。其三〈夜間行歌〉，[†]則是我所謂的舞蹈詩劇，將詩與舞蹈和戲劇表演結合在一起，自創的一種舞臺表演樣式。二十多年前，我還在中國的時候，曾為旅美的舞蹈家江青女士寫過一個這類的舞蹈節目，取材於宋代詞人李清照的〈聲聲慢〉。這些作品不同戲劇舞蹈便同電影聯繫在一起，只有〈遊神與玄思〉算個例外。

我的詩都回歸口語，一聽就懂，應該說沒有一句要費心琢磨的，哪怕我寫的時候一再修改，有的甚至改上若干年。這並非誇張，也因為我對詩歌的語言有種頗為極端的要求，得琅琅上口，甚至可以唱誦，因而首先注重的是語感和語言的樂感。對我來說，語言得出自活人的聲音，書寫與修辭是隨後的事。換句話說，不以文害意，造成語障，這種苛求又來自我對現代漢語的反思。現代漢語的歐化，把西方語言的

---

† 詩劇〈夜間行歌〉的英譯者為陳順妍，譯本載高行健的 *City of the Dead and Song of the Night*（香港中文大學出版社，2015。譯者：方梓勳、陳順妍）。〈夜間行歌〉的英譯本並未收進本書。

Let us also consider the five major pieces in this book. First, "I Say Hedgehog" is more of a tease; I call it a modern folk song because, nowadays, folk songs have been displaced by pop songs. Second, "As Carefree as a Bird" was originally written for a movie. In that movie, I managed to break away from the narrative format of film and classed the movie as filmic poetry. Third, "Song of the Night"[†] is what I call poetic dance drama, which blends poetry, dance, and play, and, as a result, I created a new style of stage performance. Twenty years ago, when I was still in China, I wrote a similar dance program for Ms. Jiang Qing, who was then based in the U.S. The work was derived from a *ci* poem called "A Slow Slow Tune" by the Song Dynasty poet Li Qingzhao (1084–1155). All these works were either related to dance drama or to film. The only exception is "Wandering Mind and Metaphysical Thoughts."

All my poems represent a return to spoken language. As soon as you hear them, you should be able to understand their meaning. There is no need for studious analysis, even though, when I wrote, I would revise them time and again, sometimes over a period of many years. This is not an exaggeration; the reason is that I make very exacting demands on the language of each of my poems. It has to be infinitely speakable, even singable. Thus, priority is given to the feeling of language and musicality. To me, language has to come from living human beings, and writing and rhetoric only follow afterwards. In other words, we should not destroy meaning for the sake of floridity, which would result only in language barriers. Such a seemingly excessive demand also arises out of my reflections on modern Chinese. With the Europeanization of modern

---

† The poetic drama, "Song of the Night" translated by Mabel Lee is included in Gao Xingjian's *City of the Dead and Song of the Night,* translated into English by Gilbert C. F. Fong and Mabel Lee (Hong Kong: The Chinese University Press, 2015). "Song of the Night" is not included in the present collection.

語法和句法形態不加消化，生硬引入現代中文的行文，往往讀來費勁，難以聽懂。近三十年來，西方現當代文學和語言學的譯介更促使中文進一步歐化。我反其道行之，追求的是現代漢語的通達和流暢。

我以聽覺來梳理筆下的語言，通過朗讀，是凡費解的詞句一概清除。語言的語感與樂感超乎語法與修辭的範疇，同說這種語言的人活生生的感受密切相關。漢語的四聲，平上去入形成的抑揚頓挫，是中文語音語調的基本構成。古漢語主要以四字句行文，《詩經》與《楚辭》正源出於此。之後的五言與七言律詩和詞曲的格律同樣建立在四聲的基礎上，進而賦予節奏的變換，更加音韻化。

白話文為漢語引入大量的雙音和多音節詞，還有許多外來語譯成的新詞，再加上西方語言的語法和詞法的形態湧入現代漢語，中文語音語調固有的四聲似乎忽略了。我的詩則確認四聲形成的語調與由此而來的節奏，並訴諸宣敘和詠嘆，因而便於出聲朗讀。我寫作的時候時常借鑒音樂，希望詩句富於音韻和節奏感，這也是我的詩在語言上追求的方向。

Chinese, Western grammar and syntax have forced their way into Chinese writing without being properly digested. Consequently, writing became barely comprehensible and to understand it takes a lot of effort. In the last thirty years, the translation of contemporary Western literature and linguistic works has resulted in further Europeanization. I am taking an opposite path; I strive for comprehensibility and fluency when I am writing modern Chinese.

I use my ears to edit and polish my language. Through reading aloud, I eradicate all that is hard to understand. The lingual sense and the musical sense, which are beyond the realm of grammar and rhetoric, are intimately related to the living human being speaking the words. The four tones of the Chinese language—the level, rising, going, and entering tones—and the cadences they bring about make up the fundamentals of the sounds and intonations of poetry. Ancient Chinese poetry is usually written in four-character clusters. *The Book of Poetry* and *The Song of Chu* were written according to this format. The metrical pattern of the five-character and seven-character poems that came later was also based on the four tones, which gives the lines rhythm and variation to make them more phonetically pleasing.

Modern standard Chinese has introduced a large number of bi-syllabic and multi-syllabic word groups and neologisms from other parts of the world. Furthermore, Western grammar and syntax have flooded into the Chinese language, and the four-tone system of the Chinese language appears to have been neglected. My poems, on the other hand, affirm the intonation formed by the four tones and the rhythm that they produce. I also resort to recitation, singing, and chanting; thus, they are easily read aloud. When I write, I always rely on music, and I also borrow from it, hoping that my poems are imbued with the appropriate rhyme and rhythm. This is the goal I strive to achieve in the language of my poetry.

二十世紀西方現代詩的大趨勢是結束抒情，文藝復興以來歐洲詩歌的這一深厚的傳統已經消失。從法語阿波里奈爾宣告的超現實主義，到英語艾略特的《荒原》的反抒情，在詩歌創作領域裏確認了現代性這一美學宗旨。詩同歌於是分家，詞與詩意也分道揚鑣，恰如造型藝術中美的消逝，代之以形式或觀念。現如今，這現代性原本作為革新的時代性標誌，也已蛻變為空洞的美學教條，而詩意何在？對詩歌創作而言倒是個真問題。

誠然，中文詩歌自有悠久的傳統，又以詩言志和意境說為兩大分野。西方的現代詩進入漢語較之白話詩還要再晚幾十年。是中學為體還是洋為中用，這類空泛的討論對現今的中文詩創作應該說絲毫無補。詩人們在自己的創作中自然各有追求。我的詩如果說也有個趨向的話，那就是在這商品拜物教和政治無孔不入的時代，去找尋已經喪失了的詩意，恰如我正準備拍攝的電影詩《美的葬禮》，企圖通過對美的哀悼而發出呼喚：回歸人性，回到審美，於無意義中尋求含意，通過觀審喚醒良知，希冀多少捕捉到詩意的一點蹤跡。

2011年11月10日於巴黎

In the 20th century, the trend in modern Western poetry was to move away from lyricism. This deeply rooted and rich tradition of European poetry had already dissipated since the Renaissance. From the surrealism proclaimed by Guillaume Apollinaire to the anti-lyricism in T. S. Eliot's *The Waste Land*, poetry had come to affirm modernity as its aesthetic aim, thus separating itself from songs; words and poetic feeling also parted company. In the same way, beauty in the plastic arts died, its place taken by form and concept. Nowadays, modernity, which had originally designated a time of revolution and change, was itself transformed into an empty and meaningless aesthetic doctrine. Where, then, is poetry? This is the real question facing poetic writing.

As we all know, there is a long tradition of Chinese poetry. There are two motivations behind the writing of poetry, to express the will and to describe a feeling, or "poetic realm." The introduction of Western modernist poetry occurred a few decades later than the emergence of poetry written in the Chinese vernacular. As for the controversy between Chinese learning as substance and Western learning for practical use, it is not at all useful in the writing of Chinese poetry nowadays. Poets invariably pursue their own goals in their creations. If one were to identify a trend in my poetry, one could probably say that I am searching for a poetic feeling, which has been long lost in this age of the ubiquitous presence of commodification, materialism, and politics. Just like what I am attempting to do in my upcoming filmic poem, *Requiem for Beauty*, I try to issue a call to arms through my eulogy for Beauty: return to human nature and aesthetics, look for meaning among meaninglessness, and awaken conscience through observation. In this manner, we could hopefully capture at least some traces of poetic feeling.

Paris, 10th November 2011

《失落的記憶》 *The Lost Memory*
2009, 240cm × 225cm.

遊神與玄思

Wandering Mind and Metaphysical Thoughts

《欣悦》 *Enchantment*
2011, 98cm × 130cm.

《草圖・三》 *Drawing III*
1996, 21cm × 15cm.

《草圖・八》　*Drawing VIII*
1996, 21cm × 15cm.

我説刺蝟

(現代歌謠)

刺蝟
我説
一條蟲
慢慢流淌

十七年前
科羅拉多
有一條河
沒魚美人
並非不幸

基督孤獨
孤獨的基督

黃昏
昏黃
草原
瘋長的草原的風

一隻破鞋
和
一個孩子
遺忘了……

甚麼？
有一天
下雨

I Say Hedgehog

(A Modern Folk Song)

Hedgehog
I say
A worm
Flowing slowly

Seventeen years ago
In Colorado
There was a river
No mermaids
But not unfortunate

Jesus Christ was alone
The lonely Jesus Christ

Yellow dusk
Dusky yellow
Meadow
Crazy, long winds on the meadow

A broken shoe
And
A child
Forgotten....

What?
That day
It rained

她說
要個孩子
還要
別墅
好度假

假如都是真的
神話
比情話更燙

世界
破成無數碎片
拾不起來

蟬翼
顫顫

風
有息無聲
從腳心透骨髓

女人
手指修長
冷眼
觀看她那作品

他
喃喃吶吶
講述一長串故事
全都沒有的事

She said
She wanted a child
She also wanted
A villa
For her holiday

If they were real
Myths
Would be hotter than love talk

The world
Into countless pieces
Shattered
Can't be picked up

Cicada wings
Quivering, quivering

The wind
Air without sound
From the foot soles to the bone marrow

A Woman
Slender fingers
Cold eyes
Looking at her work

He
Murmuring and muttering
Tells a long series of stories
Which never took place

語言
漿糊
禁忌和嫉妒

風
只數
脊椎骨

纖纖手指
比言語更殘酷

沒有人說得清
這顫慄
有何意義

屋頂
雨聲淅瀝

再一次
空虛

門兀自敞開
黑海幽幽
在地圖一角

一隻帆船老舊
永遠停靠
在鏡面這邊

Words
Glue
Taboos and jealousy

Wind
Counts only
Vertebrae

Slender fingers
Crueler than words

None can explain
This quiver
What does it mean

Roof
The pitter-patter of rain

One more time
Emptiness

The door swings open
The black sea
In the map's corner

A yacht, old and torn
Rests forever
On this side of the mirror

你
弄不清
也不想弄清
弄也弄不清
你還是不是你自己

荒原
一個虛假的詞

都是英雄

地鐵車站
廣告廣告
全都性商標

沒有了
開始就知道結局

沒有新聞
便製造一個

他
投籃
中了彩票

哈哈大笑
不為甚麼
只因為無聊

You
Can't make it clear
And don't want to make it clear
Even if you tried, you couldn't make it
clear
Whether you are still you

Waste land
A falsehood

All are heroes

Metro station
Advertisements, advertisements
All sex logos

No more
Already know the ending at the
beginning

No news
Make one piece

He
Shoots at the basket
And wins the lottery

You're roaring with laughter
Not for any reason
Just because you're bored

誰都抱怨鄰居

把字拆開
人
便也無法辨認

將句子搓洗
如同打麻將
再
長長短短
排成詩行

倫理
弄進洗衣機裏
攪乎一遍
一場革命
近乎完成

屋頂塌陷
雨
落在
裸體
擰絞一起

鐘擺盪到至高點
徑自落下

最大限度消費
男女都一樣
平等的意義

Everyone complains about their neighbors

When a word is dismantled
People
Cannot recognize it

Shuffle the words
Like when playing mahjong
Then
Some long, some short
Arrange them into poetic lines

Ethics
Put them into a washing machine
Agitate them for a while
A revolution
It's almost done

The roof has collapsed
Rain
Falls on
Naked bodies
Curled into a bundle

The pendulum swings to its amplitude
It falls down by itself

Maximum consumption
Men and women are the same
The meaning of equality

精神在鏡子裏面

一棵樹
草場前
雨霧迷濛

蛙鳴
深處

純詩安在？

語言金字塔廢墟
爬出條蜥蜴
尾巴斷了

夏天溫涼
還是夏天嗎？

十七
一個最沒有意義的數字

偶然並非偶然
又非必然
形式之規定
恰如命運

此時此刻
交合與感覺
如此而已

The spirit resides in a mirror

A tree
In front of the meadow
Rain and fog, misty

A frog croaks
In the deep

Where is pure poetry?

Language, pyramid, ruin
Out crawls a lizard
Its tail snapped

Cool Summer
Still Summer?

Seventeen
A most meaningless number

Accidents are not accidental
And they're not inevitable
Forms are regulated
Just like fate

At this moment
Intercourse and feeling
Nothing more

時間不過是機遇
留不下痕迹
只有記憶

最後一班地鐵
微微顫動窗玻璃
穿過海灣

乳房
一道傷痕

不許說
不等於沒說

沒有明天
沒有
沒有

一顆黑痣
一頭傻驢
都是混蛋

解脱了紐扣
解脱了虛偽
解脱了負擔
只剩下疲倦

童年像只老猫
在椅墊上打盹

Time is nothing but opportunity
Leaving no trace
Only memories

The last metro
Lightly shaking the window glass
Darting across the bay

Breast
A scar

Being prohibited from speaking
It's not the same as not saying it

No tomorrow
No
No

A black mole
A silly donkey
Both are bastards

Undo the buttons
Undo hypocrisy
Undo the burden
All that's left is weariness

Childhood is like an old cat
It yawns on the cushion

你開始講述說了一千遍的故事
一千零一夜只有那零頭還有點
　意思

魔鬼騎在牆上
用鞭子抽打
一匹母馬

魔鬼就是你！

那母馬
名字
叫
我們大家

都追趕時髦
生怕落伍

你寧可回到鄉間集市
去喝早茶

再說
說甚麼？
一個笑話
牙
老掉了

蝴蝶為甚麼不是別的？
只因為蝴蝶是蝴蝶

You begin to tell a story told a
thousand times before
In one thousand and one nights only the
small change is remotely meaningful

The devil sits on the wall
He cracks the whip and lashes
A mare

The devil is you!

The mare
Its name
Is called
All of us

All chase after fashion
Afraid of falling behind

You'd rather go back to the market in the
country
To have morning tea

What's more
What's there to say?
A joke
Teeth
Fallen out because of old age

Why are butterflies not something else?
Only because butterflies are butterflies

營造意象
從顏色開始
營造顏色
靠三寸不爛之舌

都拼命證明
地球是扁的
自我滾圓
真理總得圍住甚麼人
團團直轉

一架飛機
墜落在
孩子夢裏

一顆棗核
不知道發芽
不知道發芽的棗核
不知道害怕

把窗戶打開
在牆皮上塗鴉
畫隻仙鶴
嘴巴肥大

恐懼只來自不可知
知道了
便不再說話

To construct imagery
Start with color
To construct color
It relies on a silver tongue

They are all desperately trying to
  prove
That the earth is flat
By rotating it makes itself round
Truth must surround some people
For it to go round and round

An aeroplane
Crashes down
Onto a child's dream

A date pit
It doesn't know how to sprout
A date pit which doesn't know how to
  sprout
Doesn't know about fear

Open the window
Draw some graffiti on the wall
Paint a red-crowned crane
With a big fat beak

Fear comes from the unknown
If you know it
You no longer talk

除了性
這世界還剩下甚麼？

除了魔鬼
還有沒有童話？

除了你
還有我嗎？

除了你之於我之我之於她
一個女人
不知道真實與否
總也在編造謊話

離開了謊言
該多麼惶恐
於是你騙我騙
把謊言加以彙編
編織一個個巢穴
做成一顆顆信念
便理也得
心也安

你打
哈欠

(1991)

Without sex
Will there still be anything left in the
  world?

Without the devil
Will there still be fairy tales?

Without you
Will there still be me?

Without you to me to me to her
A woman
Not knowing what's true or false
She's always making up lies

Without lies
You should be so frightened
Therefore, you cheat and I cheat
Making up, compiling lies
Weaving them into a nest
Fashioning them into this or that faith
You feel at ease
You have peace of mind

You give
A yawn

(1991)

《沉沒》　*The Submersion*
2008, 81cm × 60cm.

《沉思》 *Self Observation*
2008, 73cm × 60cm.

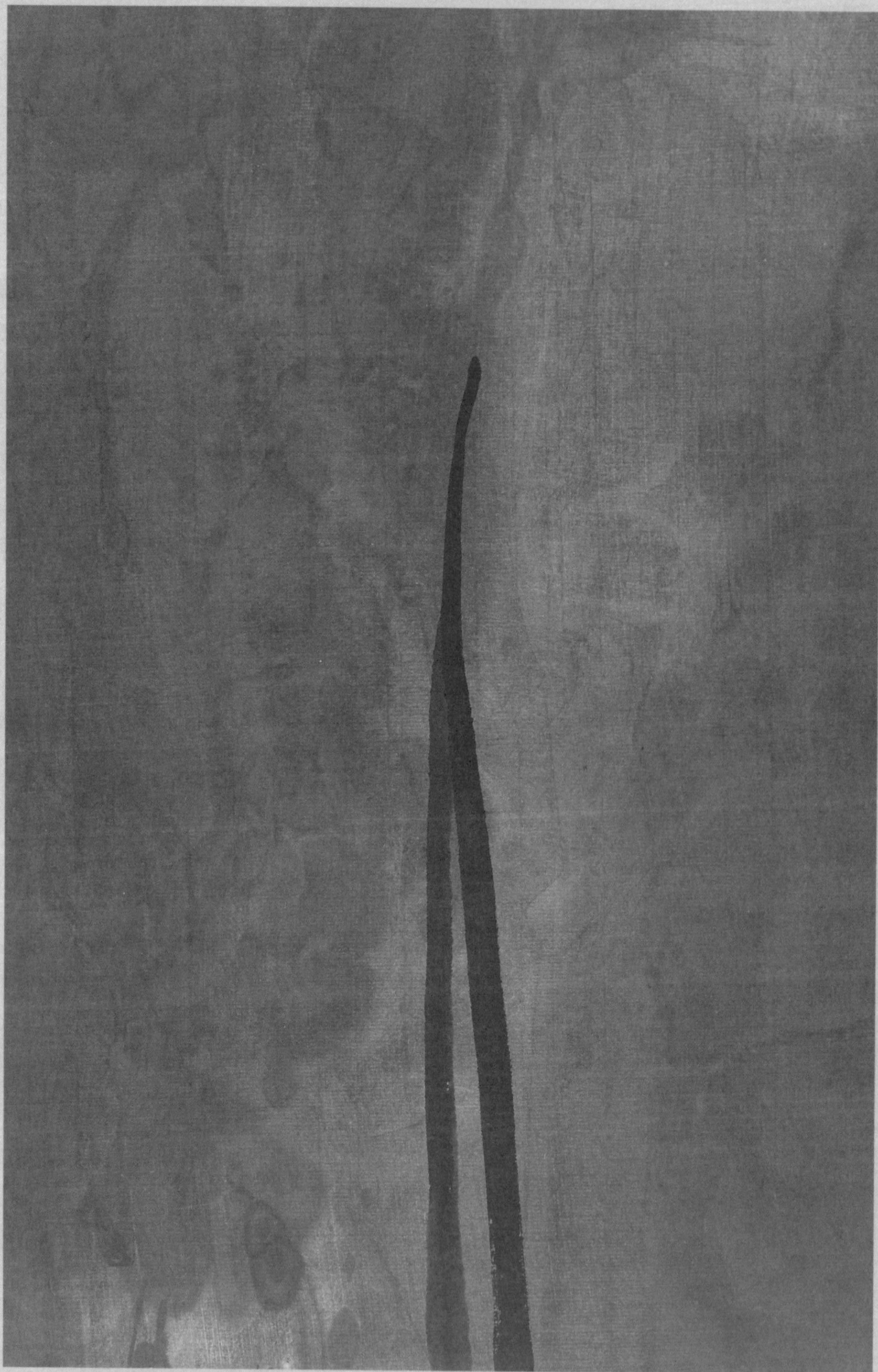

《影》 *Shadow*
1991, 54cm × 43cm.

《祈禱》 *Prayer*
2010, 66cm × 54cm.

逍遙如鳥

你若是鳥
僅僅是隻鳥
迎風即起
率性而飛
眼睜睜俯視
暗中混沌的人世

飛越泥沼
於煩惱之上
聽風展翼
這夜行毫無目的
自在而逍遙

盤旋環顧
或徑直如梭
都隨心所欲
何必再回去收拾
滿地的瑣碎

既無約束
也無顧慮
更無怨恨
往昔的重負
一旦解除
自由便無所不在

As Carefree as a Bird

If you are a bird
And nothing more than a bird
You rise with the wind
You fly as you please
With your round eyes wide open
You look down upon the earth
This dark and chaotic world of men

You fly across the mud and mire
Over all the troubles
You listen to the wind
You spread your wings
This night journey has no destination
All at ease and free of care

You circle and look around
Or shuttle-like dash in a direct line
You do as your heart pleases
There's no need to go back and tidy up
The petty things strewn all over the
ground

You've nothing tying you down
You've no remorse or regret
You're free from the past's heavy
burdens
Once they've been unloaded
Freedom is everywhere

迴旋淩空
猛然俯衝
隨即掠地滑行
都好生盡興

沉沉大地
竟跟隨你搖曳
時而起伏
時而豎立
那地平線
本遙不可及
頓時消失了
一個個奇景
全出乎意料

雲或是霧
一掠而過
微光和晨曦
盡收眼底

群山移動
一個湖泊在旋轉
猶如思緒
你優遊在
海與曠漠之間
晝與夜交匯處

You circle high above the sky
Suddenly, you take a dive
And glide along the face of the earth
Enjoying yourself to the full

The earth is hefty and heavy
But it sways with you
At times it surges, up and down
At times it stands upright
The horizon down below
It might be visible but can't be reached
Suddenly it vanishes into naught
Wonderful sights appear one after
  another
Totally out with expectations

Maybe it's cloud
Maybe it's fog
Past it sweeps in a flash
The shimmering light and the morning sun
All come into sight

The mountains are moving
In circles, a lake is turning
Just like the thoughts in your mind
Freely, leisurely, wandering
Between the vast desert and the ocean
At the meeting point of night and day

偌大一隻慧眼
引導你前去
未知之境

憑這目光
你便如鳥
從冥想中升騰
消解詞語的困頓
想像都難以抵達
那模糊依稀之處
霎時間在眼前
一一浮現

玄思的意境
無遠無近
也沒有止盡
清晰而光明

明晃晃一片光亮
空如同滿
令永恆與瞬間交融
時光透明
而若干陰影與裂痕
從中湧現某種遺忘

這一切從未見過
瞬息變化
難以預料
稍許恍惚
便喪失了

So big is the eye of wisdom
It guides you going forward
To a place unknown

With this vision
You become like a bird
Rising up from meditation
To escape the predicament of words
With difficulty does imagination arrive
At this fuzzy and hazy place
But right at this moment, in front of
  your eyes
Up it springs, one after another

The realm of metaphysical thoughts
It's neither near nor far
It's interminable
It's vivid and bright

A field of luminescent ebullience
It's empty but it's full
There merge eternity and transience
Transparent is time
From shadows and cracks
There emerges a certain forgetfulness

You've never seen any of this before
Changing in a moment
They're unpredictable
A brief absence of mind
And they'll disappear

你重又暗中徘徊
清楚的只是
你畢竟不是鳥
也解不脱
這無所不在
總糾纏不息
日常的紛擾

一番徒勞
得找個避風港
安撫你的靈魂
倘若這魂魄
你或許還有
可不該有個去處
既非天堂
也非地獄
令這失重
得以承受

如何找到一片淨土
讓這困擾的人生
耗盡之際
解除掉妄念
好得以安息

你可曾見過
一隻老鳥
衰弱不堪
惶恐不安
悽悽慘慘

You wander, once again, in darkness
Only one thing is clear
That, after all you're not a bird
And you cannot free yourself
From the ubiquitous
Ever entangling
Troubles of the day-to-day

In the wake of futilities
You must seek a haven
To sooth and to becalm your soul
Shouldn't this soul of yours
(Assuming you still have it)
Go and find a place somewhere
That is neither Heaven nor Hell
To lodge and support
This weightless sensation

Where to find a stretch of Pure
  Land?
So that this troubled life
Arrived at a time of total
  exhaustion
Can shed all delusions
And gain some peace of mind

Have you ever seen
An aged bird
A frail, and weak, and feeble bird
Terrified and ill at ease
Desolate and heartbroken

哀怨
哭泣
乞求
苟延殘喘？

是鳥都知道
優遊了一生
時間來臨
便徑自奉上
作為祭品

是鳥都找好
隱匿之地
垂危之際
靜靜等候
生命消逝
這聖地莫不
也是你的歸宿
又在何處？

(2009)

Whining
Wailing
Begging
At its final gasp?

Any bird would've known
All of its life has been leisurely,
  carefree
When the time has come
It offers itself
As a sacrifice

Any bird would've found
A hiding place
When it's at death's door
Quietly, there, awaiting the moment
When life vanishes
This hallowed ground
If it isn't also your final resting place
Where else could it be?

(2009)

《夢中的房屋》 *The Dreamed House*
2011, 130cm × 97cm.

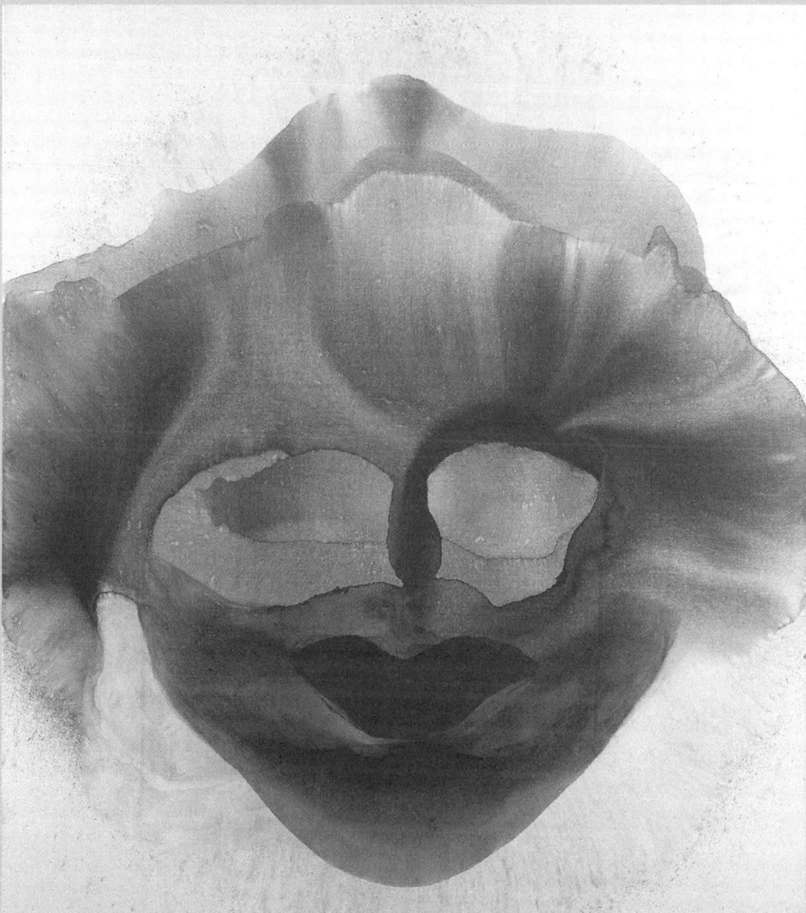

《人生如戲》 *The Mask*
2011, 100cm × 100cm.

遊神與玄思

(1)

生命之於你
重又變得這般新鮮
還在這人世
縱情盡性
再一番馳騁
莫大的幸運！

死神本當將你收拾
是上帝說且慢
再留他一程
這孽障猶言未盡
不妨由他把話説完

這主太多的頭腦
早該清理掉
與陰暗為伍的死神
如是説

上帝畢竟仁慈
放他一馬
待他如寵兒
再一次寬容

Wandering Mind and Metaphysical Thoughts

(1)

Life to you
Has become so new and fresh again
You're still alive in the world of men
You can act with abandon
Once more, you can wander around
You're so lucky!

Death tried to take you away
It was God who said
Wait, let him stay a while yet
This sinner has still not said all he
 wants to say
Let him finish what he's saying

This guy has too much brain
He should've been dealt with much
 earlier
Thus said Death
Who is always accompanied by
 Darkness

After everything, God was merciful
He let him off
He treated him like
His favorite son
And forgave him one more time

(2)
如今，你離蒼天很近
離人寰甚遠
方才贏得這份清明
啊，偌大的自在！

你俯視人世
芸芸眾生
紛紛擾擾
一片混沌
竄來竄去
全然不知
那隱形的大手
時不時暗中撥弄

(3)
井圈
無限幽深
上帝
就坐在裏面
閉目養神
你我都看不見

(4)
生命是個奇蹟
你來到人世

(2)
Now you're very close to Heaven
Far away from the world of men
Just now can you achieve absolute clarity
O, what a feeling of freedom and peace!

You look down at humanity, now at your feet
The multitude of faces
Hustling and bustling
A prodigious mass of confusion and chaos
People scurry here and there
Altogether unaware
That the unseen, giant hand
Will manipulate their fates, in secret, now and then

(3)
The well shaft
Deep, dark, and bottomless
And God
Sitting inside the shaft
Closes His eyes to rest
He sees neither you nor me

(4)
Life is a miracle
Your arrival in this world of men

純屬偶然
你其實
不如一根草
是否過得了今冬
只有天知道
那草明春
照樣風中飄搖

你如此渺小
還不如塵埃
限期到了
便一筆勾銷
可塵埃呢
去而復來
總也抹不掉

生命來得偶然
去也偶然
靈魂的消散
比塵埃還快
塵土與生命
原本分不清
昇華與還原
無所謂終極
你便是一個
不可言說的奇蹟

It's purely an accident
In fact
You're no more than a blade of grass
Whether or not you can survive this
  Winter
Only Heaven knows
But, come next Spring, the wind will
  ripple
That blade of grass as before

You're small
Even smaller than a dust speck
When your time comes
You'll be wiped out
But dust
No matter the number of times you
  wipe it away
It'll still be there

Life comes by accident
It also goes by accident
The soul disperses
Faster than dust
Dust and life
They were the same, in the beginning
Sublimation, restoration
There's no so-called ending
You're one of them
The ineffable miracles

(5)
一顆骷髏
兩個黑洞
殘缺的下巴
不再說話
一副散架的骨骼
如同乾枯的樹杈

(6)
只要退後一步
便可以審視
那顆頭顱
儘管取下
盡興把玩
等膩味了
不妨再安上

(7)
真理不可說
說出的都不是
知道了就好
不知道的
可不由他去了

譬如說
人不免一死
誰聽了不是聳肩
就撇嘴一笑

(5)
A skeleton
Two black holes
A broken chin
No longer able to speak
A set of bones in disarray
Like the dried-up branches of a tree

(6)
If only you'd take one step back
You could then examine
The skeleton's head
You could take it down
Play around with it all you want
When you grow sick and tired thereof
Put it back again

(7)
The truth cannot be said
That which can be said is not the truth
It's good enough if you know
If you don't know
Just let it be

For example
Man cannot avoid death
Whoever hears this will shrug his
  shoulders
Or purse his lips and smile

到笑不了的時候
也就驗證了

(8)
要知道
你好不容易從泥沼爬出來
何必去清理身後那攤污泥
且讓爛泥歸泥沼
身後的聒噪去鼓譟
只要生命未到盡頭
儘管一步一步
走自己的路

(9)
你不妨再造
一個失重的自然
心中的伊甸園
可以任你優遊
由你盡興

(10)
須知
自言自語
乃語言的宗旨

When he can smile no longer
It's verification time.

(8)
You have to know
It was hard to worm your way out of
the mire
Why bother to clean up the dirt left
behind?
Let the dirt return to the mire
And let the row you left behind rise to
uproar
As long as your life has not reached its
end
You'll just have to take it one step at a
time
And walk on the way you've chosen

(9)
Perhaps you could try to re-create
A weightless Nature
A Garden of Eden in your heart
A place where you could freely roam
And enjoy yourself to the full

(10)
You have to know
Talking to oneself
Betokens language's essence

而遊思隨想
恰是詩的本意

(11)
上帝成了一隻青蛙
就不那麼兇狠
睜大眼睛不說話
而上帝不開口
也不那麼可怕

魔鬼便坐在你對面
同你討論人性之惡
和人的醜陋
而人心之善
卻不是魔鬼的事
說得竟那麼到位
都止不住哈哈大笑
沒有過的透徹
難得這樣開心

上帝
睜睜一隻圓眼
另一隻緊閉
默不做聲
只聽

Random and wandering thoughts
Precisely embody poetry's true nature

(11)
If God became a frog
He wouldn't be so cruel
His eyes would widen,
He would say nothing
When God keeps His mouth shut
He becomes not so terrifying

Then the Devil sits opposite you
And talks to you of the evil nature of
man
And of his ugliness
As for his goodness
It has nothing to do with the Devil
His talk is so to the point
You can't help laughing out loud
You have never been so blessed with
clarity
Seldom have you been so happy

God
Opens one of His round eyes
Closes the other
He makes no sound
He only listens

(12)
這一切怎樣開始的
你已經記不清
總之
上帝與魔鬼
同你坐在一起
說坐不很恰當
這失重的天堂
坐或站或倒立
都沒有意義
而意在言外
說與不說如同沉默
討論便如此這般進行

上帝、魔鬼和人三方座談
你作為人的代表
雖無人選你
民主與多數取勝
人間這點道理
在天堂概不成立
至於推理與邏輯
注意！
說的正是：
堂堂正正的大道理
還抵不上一塊擦腳布

(12)
How did this all begin?
You can't clearly remember
At any rate
God and the Devil
They're sitting together with you
It's not proper to use the word
"sitting"
In this weightless Heaven
Whether sitting, or standing, or doing
a headstand
All of it is meaningless
Meaning is found beyond the words
Speaking out or not speaking out
It's the same as silence
The discussion is taking place in this way

So, God, the Devil, and Man are in
conference
You are Man's representative
Even though nobody chose you
Democracy, majority rule
These principles of the human world
They don't apply in Heaven
As for reasoning, as for logic
Attention!
The point is exactly like this:
A great idea of the utmost importance
Matters less than a rag for wiping your feet

須知：
伊甸園裏不穿鞋
魔鬼長一雙蹄子
上帝飄浮在雲端
赤腳的可不只有你

(13)
你可曾見過醜陋的樹？
無論高大或矮小
直長斜長
在平地或是山頂
哪怕石縫或是岩壁
再惡劣的氣候
環境哪怕再險惡
告訴我
你可曾見過
一棵醜陋的樹？

再說，你可曾見過
哪根草醜陋？
不管牆頭或瓦縫
叢生或孤單一株
風雨中飄搖
即使折斷或枯萎了
告訴我，你可曾見過
哪根草就此醜陋？

那麼，你可曾見過
哪座醜陋的山？

You have to know:
No one wears shoes in the Garden of
  Eden
The Devil has a pair of hooves
And God floats on the edge of the clouds
It's not just you who's barefooted

(13)
Have you ever seen a tree that is ugly?
Whether tall or short
Long and straight or long and slanting
On level plain or mountain top
In gaps between rocks or on the cliff
No matter how inclement the weather
Or how treacherous the surroundings
Tell me
Have you ever seen
A tree that is ugly?

One more thing, have you ever seen
A blade of grass that is ugly?
Whether on the wall-top or in between
  tiles
In a clump or by itself
Swaying in a storm
Even if it's snapped or dried
Tell me, have you ever seen
A blade of grass that is ugly?

And have you ever seen
An ugly mountain

荒山野嶺或林木茂盛
即使山石嶙峋
且別說崇山峻嶺
告訴我，你可曾見過
一座山醜陋？

或者，你可曾見過
醜陋的石頭？
即使打鑿或斷裂了
那怕碾得粉碎
總還保持石頭的本色

可你我無疑都見過
行徑醜陋的人
五官俱全
相貌端正
卻內心陰暗
手段兇狠
哪怕裝得一本正經
冠冕堂皇道貌岸然
做出的事卻令人跌碎眼鏡

A barren mountain or one covered
with luxuriant trees
Even if it's rocky and bald
Let alone one tall and majestic
Tell me, have you ever seen
A mountain that is ugly?

Or have you ever seen
An ugly rock?
It may have been chiseled and
snapped,
Or even shattered into pieces
It still retains its true color

But you and I have no doubt seen
People of ugly deeds
They may have regular facial features
And they may even be good-looking
But they have darkness and evil in their
hearts
The means they use are ruthless and
cruel
They may pretend to be proper and
prim
Looking honorable and upright
But they're capable of things beyond
belief

(14)
人都會說三道四
指鹿為馬
人都會對天發誓
給別人畫地為牢
人都會裝神弄鬼
較之巫師跳大神
還不那麼費氣力

人都會指東道西
品頭論足
而撒謊扯皮
較之玩魔術
來得全不費力氣

人都會扮成天使
把對方説成魔鬼
人都會口蜜腹劍
血口噴他人一身

人都會義憤填膺
正義得簡直不行
既主持了公道
又把別人踩倒

(14)
Everyone could say this and that
They'll point at a deer and say it's a
  horse
They'll swear to Heaven
They'll draw a circle and make a
  prison for others
They'll set up all sorts of plots and
  schemes
Compared to the shamans' sorcery
Their task is so much easier

Everybody loves to tittle-tattle
They'll criticize and find faults with
  everything
They'll wrangle and lie
Compared to magic tricks
Their scams are pieces of cake

Everyone could disguise themselves as
  angels
And say that others are devils
They'll coat their poison with sugar
Then spray people with blood from
  their bloody mouths

Everyone could be full of moral anger
Their righteousness filled to the brim
They will judge fairly and squarely
But they'll also walk all over others

人都會辱罵
歇斯底里發洩
一生的怨氣
誰碰上誰倒楣

人都會發瘋
還不可抑制
把對方撲倒在地
恨不能一把了結
捏住的那條活生生的性命

人都好爭鬥
這才有輸贏
還總也要打仗
容不得太平
非弄個你死我活不可
方才甘心
啊，人啊人，
不吸取教訓
從古至今永遠有戰爭
啊，不幸的人們！

(15)
和魔鬼結伴
有多輕鬆

Everyone knows how to yell at people
Seeking the hysterical release
From a lifetime's grievances
Whoever gets hit is down on his luck

Everyone could go mad
They cannot be stopped
They'll pounce upon rivals and push them down on the floor
They cannot wait to finish them in one go
And squeeze the daylight out of their lives

Everyone loves to fight
Only then will there be winners and losers
And so there must be wars
And peace has no place to stand
They must fight to the finish
And only then be reconciled
Men, oh men
You never learn your lessons
There have always been wars from the times of old
Oh men, how unlucky you are!

(15)
To make friends with the Devil
It's a piece of cake

以你做人的經驗
想像不出能那樣開心
就瞧他一路惡作劇
弄得雞飛狗跳
小兒哇哇的直哭
姑娘們尖叫
男人一張張鐵青的臉
唯有老娘們捂面
止不住竊笑
充其量也就如此而已

與魔鬼為伍毫不費心思
無須提防背後的詭計
且不説惡言中傷
暗箭傷人
僅僅是誹謗
就得一籮筐一籮筐裝
還別説種種罪名
都名正言順
大義凜然
宣判你無期徒刑

With your limited life experience
You can't imagine the happiness
Look at him, he plays tricks all the time
Wreaking havoc everywhere
Babies cry out loud
Girls scream and shriek
And the men's faces all turn livid and
  blue
The old women only are unfazed
They cover their faces and cannot stop
  snickering
That's the only thing they could
  manage to do.

You don't have to worry when you're
  with the Devil
You need no protection from back-
  handed ploys
Forget for a moment the sniping and
  mudslinging
Or the stab in the back
Defamations and slanders
They assuredly come by the bucket
And then there are charges and
  accusations
All right-sounding and proper
Inspiring awe by upholding justice
They sentence you, then, to life in
  prison

將你從故國的花名冊上
一筆勾掉

同人結伴可不是鬧著玩
再説人還不肯同你為伍
純潔隊伍先把你清除
不只是你這人
哪怕你隱蔽的思想
也統統埋葬

還是同魔鬼打交道
來得輕鬆
説笑都一無忌諱
從主席到總統的醜聞
再説到女人裙衩之間
那可是魔鬼的拿手好戲
自然津津樂道
笑得滿地打滾

這原本是魔鬼的性情
不像上帝一本正經
手持無上權柄
脾氣卻來得古怪

And from the old country's member-
ship register
Your name is promptly erased

Be careful when you choose your
partners
Besides, they may not be willing to be
your friends
A cleansing team will get rid of you
first
Not only your body
Your hidden thoughts too
All of them consigned to the grave

To deal with the Devil is easier
There's no need for concern about
cracking a joke
From chairmen and presidents'
scandals
To what lies under the skirts of women
It's all the Devil's forte
He'll readily talk all about it with
relish
While laughing and rolling all over the
floor

That's what the Devil's about,
primarily
Unlike stern and humorless God
With supreme authority in His hand
He has an erratic temper

動不動降瘟疫與天災
叫人類險些滅種
魔鬼嘛只不過
時不時鬧點荒淫

(16)
你已經千遍萬遍
追究過生命的涵義
此時此刻方才明白
這美好的瞬間
和瞬間的美妙

政客去追逐權力
準政客追蹤妄想
你毅然決然
拒絕充當他人的擺設
不再浪費所剩無多的性命
再說，這哪是你玩的遊戲

不如回到性靈所在
重建內心的造化
率性畫上個圓圈
再後退一步
將生存轉化為關注

Prescribes pestilence easily, and natural
disasters
Nearly making humans extinct
As for the Devil, he merely
Indulges himself, now and then, in
debauchery

(16)
Thousands of times
You've inquired into life's meaning
You've just begun to understand
The moment of beauty
And the beauty of the moment

Politicians scramble for power
Would-be politicians chase after pipe
dreams
With resolution, you refuse
To be other people's decoration
And waste your life, which will soon
run out
Then again, how could that ever have
been the game?

Better to return to the realm of the
spirit
Rebuild the nature of the heart
Follow your instinct, paint a circle
And then to step back
Transform existence into observation

睜開另一隻慧眼
把對象作為審美

(17)
你歌唱清風
也歌唱苦難
唱清晨和黃昏的太陽
唱早春三月
煙雨洗不淨灰濛濛的天
歌唱愛情
也歌唱失戀
還歌唱孤寂
自言自語
自己得趣

(18)
泥沼漫漫
無邊無際
沒有白天
沒有黑夜
無日無月
沒有蟲鳴
沒有鳥叫
有的只是
泥沼在呱噪
還緊緊咬住
你每一步下腳
總也擺脱不掉

And open the other eye of wisdom
To look at Beauty as the object of
study

(17)
You sing of the cooling breezes
And of suffering, you sing
Of the sun at dawn and at evening
And of March and the early Spring
The grayish sky
That can't be cleaned
With misty rain
You sing about love
And the loss of love
And also solitude
You talk to yourself
So pleased with what you're doing

(18)
The mire extends
Boundless and interminable
There's no day
There's no night
No sun, no moon
No insects humming
No chirping birds
Only the quacking of the mire
It places a tight grip
On every step you make
There isn't a way to shake it off

(19)
事情可不就這樣荒腔走板
像時間一樣扭曲
全都認不出來了
李四和張三
蚊子和蘋果
果樹或鐵犁
剃刀和刺刀
和烏鴉或蝴蝶
革命與反革命
或反革命與革命
也不知誰反誰正
邏輯與悖論
啊，唯有生命
才值得肯定
更何況
人也只能有一回

(20)
從質疑到挑戰
再導致
同世界和解
與他人共存
人生之路
大抵還只能如此

(21)
等待的往往不來
來的卻令人愕然

(19)
And so things have gone out of key
Twisted like time
You can't tell them apart
Be they Tom, Dick, or Harry
Mosquito or apple
Fruit tree or iron plow
Razor blade or bayonet
Crow or butterfly
Revolution or counter-revolution
Or counter-revolution or revolution
Don't know who's for or who's against
Logic or paradox
O, only life itself
Is worth affirming
Not to mention that
Man lives only once

(20)
From questioning to challenging
Which leads to
Reconciliations among all the nations
And, with others, peaceful
  co-existence
Perhaps the road of life
Can only be like that

(21)
What you're waiting for never comes
When it comes, it's so unexpected

烏托邦最好永遠
留在烏有之鄉

希望之虛妄
不如實實在在
過一天是一天
一如既往

(22)
號角響了
遠遠來自天邊
像一層層波浪
悠長悠長
由遠及近
傳遞到跟前
喚起心中
深深的悸動

天也黎明
你該啓程
這行程等了整整一生
沒有預定的路線
也沒有目的
還沒有終點

你伸出左手
不，你伸出右手

Better to let Utopia
Stay in nowhereland forever

Hope is nothing but a pipe dream
Might as well be realistic
And live from one day to another
Just like we have always done

(22)
The horn has sounded
Far away, over the horizon
Like waves, layer upon layer
The sound lasts a long time
Coming nearer from far away
It delivers itself beneath your feet
Arousing in your heart
Deep poundings

Day has broken
You'd better start your journey
A journey you've awaited all your
  life
There's no planned itinerary
There isn't any purpose
Nor is there any destination

You extend your left hand
No, it's your right hand

閉上雙眼
徑直向前
這就是你要走的路
你要走出的路
其實就在腳底

居然還有一生
且不管長短
供你消遣
又多麼幸運

(23)
你如此脆弱
如同石縫中一根草
居然踩不死

你如此微小
如同一粒種子
卻無處不能生根

你守住內心
那清明的意識
人世眾生相
看在眼裏
世間的糾葛
概不理會

Closing your eyes
You proceed straight ahead
This is the way you want to go
The way you want to make for
  yourself
It's right under your feet

You actually have a life to live
No matter if it's long or short
It's for you to spend
How lucky you are!

(23)
You're so fragile
Like a blade of grass between rocks
Surprisingly surviving repeated
  trampling

You are so tiny
Like a single seed
That could take root anywhere

You carefully guard the inner depth of
  your mind
That limpid consciousness
The myriad phenomena of life
You watch them with your eyes
The world's conflicts, on the other hand
You ignore them all

你自我審視
明鏡之中
另有一番境界
也就了卻妄念
抵達一個人
所能的極限

(24)
從兒時起
一生的努力
那永無止境的義務
而責任又一再追加
壓得你難以喘息
如今剩下這點時間
該留給自己

不妨把一輪明月
托在掌心
或是凝望海天之際
橙紅的太陽正在下沉
闔上眼睛
去追隨落日的餘暉

(25)
如今沒有人對你發號施令
沒有人賦予你甚麼使命
沒有人期待你的聲音

You examine yourself closely
In the bright mirror
There exists a different realm
You banish all delusions
And arrive at the ultimate
Of where a person can go

(24)
Since childhood
You've been working hard all your life
The never-ending obligations
The responsibilities keep adding up
They weigh you down
You find it difficult breathing
Now you have only this little time left
That you should keep for yourself

You'd rather place the bright full
moon
In the center of your palm
Or gaze at the edge of the sea
At the point where it meets the sky
When the orange sun is sinking low
Close your eyes
Follow the lingering, setting light

(25)
Now no one orders you around
Nobody gives you a mission
No one looks forward to hearing your
voice

你居然有話要說
還非說不可
不能不說的話
才訴諸筆墨

(26)
啊，詩
無非語言的遊戲
思想
才是語言的要義
啊，以詩言志
又多麼乏味

你不如以言語戲弄人世
可別忘記且先愉悅自己

(27)
我沉重而你飄拂
我混濁而你清明

我狹隘而你豁達
我自以為是
你無是無非

你平靜而我躁動
你注視之下
我幸好得以沉靜

But you've actually something to say
And you have to say it
The things you can't help saying
You put them in writing

(26)
Ah, poetry
Nothing but a game of language
It is thinking
Which is the essence of language
Ah, if poetry is to "express one's will"
How boring it would be!

You would rather tease the world with words
But don't forget to please yourself first

(27)
I'm heavy, you're light and airy
I'm cloudy, you're clear

I'm narrow-minded, you're magnanimous
I'm opinionated
You're open to all suggestions

You're calm, I'm restless
Under your watchful eyes
Luckily I can have some peace of mind

(28)
你一個遊人
無牽無掛
沒有家人
沒有故鄉
無所謂祖國
滿世界遊蕩

你沒有家族
更無門第
也無身分
孑然一身
倒更像人

你如風無形
無聲如影
無所不在

你
僅僅是一個指稱
一旦提及
霎時面對面
便在鏡子裏邊

(29)
啊你
一個優人
嘻嘻哈哈
調笑這世界

(28)
You're a wanderer
You have no worries
No family
No hometown
No so-called motherland
You keep on roaming all over the
world

You have neither clan nor family
No pedigree, of course
And no identity
You have no one
But that's more human

You're invisible like the wind
Silent like a shadow
You're ubiquitous

You
It's merely a reference
Once the reference is made
Instantly you're face-to-face with
yourself
Inside the mirror

(29)
Ah, you
You are an actor
Laughing and joking
Making fun of this world

遊戲人生
全不當真

哦，你
一個悠人
悠哉游哉
無所事事
一無執著
無可無不可

嘿，你
好一個幽人
在社會邊緣
人際之間
那種種計較
概不沾邊

(30)
你
一團意識
清晰而澄明
而我混沌之際
霎時間
便離我而去

你
說來便來
毫不含糊

Life to you is a game
You never regard it as real

Oh, you
You're an idler
You take things easy
You do nothing
You never insist
You don't care one way or the other

Hey, you
What a recluse!
You live on the margins of society
What happens between one person
  and another
Their many schemes and many
  squabbles
You refuse to have anything to do with
  them

(30)
You
You're a big mass of consciousness
Clear and limpid
At the time of chaos
In a split second
You depart and leave me behind

You
You come as you wish
Unequivocally

說去便去
更無猶豫

你
說有便有
說無便無
超越生命的短暫

你
無生無死
不生不滅

你
看不見的光
聽不見的聲音
可近可遠
咫尺到無限

你永恆
而我
不過是個過客

(31)
感覺到的
詩人才說
感覺不到的
留給哲學

(32)
該說的似乎已經說了
剩下的不可言說

You go as you wish
Without hesitation

You
You exist if you say so
You don't exist if you don't
You transcend the transience of life

You
You have no birth and no death
You have neither life nor extinction

You
You are the light that can't be seen
The voice that can't be heard
You could be far or near
Close by or at infinity-and-beyond

You are eternity
But me
I'm just a passer-by

(31)
Only that which can be felt
That, the poet will talk about
That which can't be felt
Let's leave it to philosophy

(32)
I've said all that I ought to say
What's left could not be said

也就不必說穿
不妨學佛陀
咧嘴
做一副笑臉

(33)
從說完了的地方下筆
畫一塊石頭深思
畫棵柳樹悲泣
再畫一隻不流淚的眼睛
注視你自己

(34)
偶然來到人世
又偶然走了
命運之於人
或人之於命運
可不如此

(35)
沒有怨恨
又多麼輕鬆
七十而立
還穩穩當當
撿回剩下不多的性命
誠然
你抗拒不了死亡
只是同死神一再周旋
以遊戲延緩他的來臨

No need to expose anything
Might as well imitate Buddha
With his mouth in a big grin
He puts on a smiling face

(33)
Start to write from the end
Paint a rock to meditate
Paint a willow to wail and cry
Then paint an eye which has no tears
Gaze at yourself

(34)
You came to this world by accident
And by accident you'll be gone
How fate affects man
Or how man affects his fate
It's all the same

(35)
No hatred
How relaxing
You're seventy and you stand firm
Still steady and sound
Pick up what's left of your life
It's true
You can't fight Death
But again and again I tussled with
  Death
Playing games to put off his arrival

(36)
你又見到那人
夜半三更
一身黑衣
孑然一身
瘦骨伶仃
不緊不慢
飄拂如風
好一副身形
猶如無主的影子
在這世上遊蕩
又像一個隱喻
或一則寓言

(2010)

(36)
You see that man again
In the middle of the night
Dressed in black
All alone
Skinny and scrawny
Not fast, not slow
He drifts lightly as the wind
What a fine physique
Like a shadow without an owner
He keeps wandering through the world
Or like a metaphor
Or a fable

(2010)

《美的葬禮》圖 1 *Requiem for Beauty* Image 1
2013

《美的葬禮》圖 2　*Requiem for Beauty* Image 2
2013

《美的葬禮》圖 3　*Requiem for Beauty* Image 3
2013

《美的葬禮》圖 4　*Requiem for Beauty* Image 4
2013

《美的葬禮》圖 5　*Requiem for Beauty* Image 5
2013

美的葬禮

(電影詩)

(1)
你是否知道美已經消逝？
甚麼？說甚麼？
你是否知道美已經死亡？
不明白說的甚麼？
你是否知道美已經葬送掉？
這怎麼可能？
要知道美就這樣了結了！

現如今　滿世界
目光所及　鋪天蓋地
處處是廣告
恰如病毒　無孔不入
每一分　每一秒
只要一打開電腦
堵都堵不住！

再不就是政治的喧鬧
黨爭和選票
而八卦氾濫
媚俗加無聊
唯獨美卻成了禁忌

Requiem for Beauty

(Filmic Poetry)

(1)

Do you know that Beauty has vanished?
What was that? What did you say?
Do you know that Beauty is already
  dead?
Don't understand, what are you talking
  about?
Do you know that Beauty has been
  annihilated?
How could that be possible?
Listen, Beauty is no more, just like that!

In this day and age, all over the world
High and low, as far as the eye can see
Nothing but ubiquitous advertisements
They've filled, like viruses, every nook
  and cranny
Every second, every minute
The moment you turn on your
  computer, there they are
They're unstoppable!

Or there's a noisy political racket
Party feuds and battles for votes
Overabundance of gossip
Inanity and kitsch
Only Beauty has become a taboo

無聲無息
了無蹤跡

你還無法知道誰幹的勾當
光天化日之下好生猖狂
美就這樣扼殺了
湮沒了　了結了
真令人憂傷！

解不開的惆悵
無窮無盡的沮喪
又向誰去述說？
都熟視無睹
有眼無珠
還找不到兇手
眾目睽睽下
大庭廣眾之中
美居然不見蹤影
精神的貧困滿世界瀰漫

這人世越來越嘈雜
人心卻一片荒涼
你四顧茫然
而眾人無言
難道都喪失了感覺
喚不起一絲迴響
全麻木不仁？
又怎麼能容忍？
這問也是白問

She has vanished without a sound
Without a trace

Who has committed this wrongful deed?
You have no way of finding out
So reckless, and in broad daylight
Just like that, Beauty was strangled
She's gone, finished!
Oh, the sorrow!

Relentless melancholy
Never-ending regrets
To whom should we turn?
People pay no attention
They have their eyes but they don't see
The murderer is still at large
In broad daylight
In full view of everyone
Beauty vanished without a trace
A spiritual destitution has pervaded the world

The world is getting more clamorous
People's hearts have turned wintry cold
You look around, you're at a loss
No one utters a word
Have they all lost their feelings?
No trace of a response
Have they all become numb?
How can they stand this silence?
It's futile to ask

滿街行人過往匆匆
你好生寂寞
不免湊近察看
一張張臉面
全都木然
一概視而不見
聽而不聞
不會觀雨
更不用說聽心
你於是恍然大悟
美已經從人心底
全然消逝
何等恐怖！

你真想大哭
卻沒眼淚
想找人訴說
竟沒有對象
沒有人能懂這憂傷
如此深沉
又如此沉重

(2)
儘管滿街燈火通明
車水馬龍川流不息
卻沒有一丁點人氣
這鋼筋水泥的叢林
無數玻璃的鏡面

The street is full of hurrying pedestrians
You feel so lonely
You can't help but lean in for a closer
look
You see faces, and more faces
Wooden expressions abundant
They look but they don't see
They hear but they don't listen
They don't marvel at the rain
Let alone listen to their hearts
Suddenly you've come to understand:
Beauty has completely vanished
From the depths of people's hearts
Oh, the horror!

You want to burst out crying
But you have no tears
You want to talk to someone
But you can't find a soul
No one can understand this sorrow
It runs so deep
The gravity

(2)
The street is bright and illuminated
Heavy traffic, vehicles in an unending
stream
But there's no sense of humanity
This jungle of concrete and steel
Countless glass panes

空晃晃而無人影
金融疊起的都市
在深淵中聳立

美可不就這樣
喪失了
遺忘了
真令人寂寞
哪裏再找尋往昔的華麗和歡欣？
燦爛的陽光下金碧輝煌的穹頂？
再也見不到藍湛湛的天
海水浩蕩也已污染
那身姿的優雅
情懷的瀟灑
那勾魂的倩影
動人心弦的眼神
如記憶一般遙遠

(3)
啊，義大利，威尼斯
居然還有個狂歡節盛會
活得既如此乏味
不如去沉醉一回
哪怕撿回的僅僅是
旅遊業營造的幻影

Yet no sign of people
A city built with money
Standing tall within the dark abyss

Just like that
Beauty is gone, forgotten
Oh, the loneliness
Where can we regain the happiness
and splendor of yore?
The golden vault under the brilliant
sun?
No more will we see the azure sky
Even the immense sea has been
polluted
The gracefulness of movements
The blithe spirit
The look that stirred our hearts
The exquisite image that captured our
souls
All have become as distant as
memories

(3)
Oh, Venice, oh, Italy
They actually hold a carnival for
revelry
Life is tedious and meaningless
You might as well live it all up, get
yourself drunk
Even though you only end up
With the mirages conjured by tourism

霧靄迷茫
苦雨連綿
碼頭空蕩蕩
清寂的街巷
往事如煙
連記憶也日益暗淡
夜浪拍岸
只喚起空洞的迴響

生命與死亡較量
狂歡與一臉憂傷
相遇在威尼斯街上
夜晚歌劇院的舞會
死亡第一次露面
銀面具黑大氅
就不知是不是
詩人在扮演

紅的廳堂迴旋的樓梯
罩面具的裸女捧乳獻姿
生命乃一場豪華的盛宴
又怎麼能不縱情歡唱

從廣場到街巷
三位死神結伴逡巡
高個子噘個鳥嘴

Misty fog, cloudy sky
Everlasting bitter rain
A harbor, deserted
An alley, quiet and empty
The past is like a puff of smoke
Even memories are fast fading
Waves break on the shore at night
Recalling only empty echoes

Life and Death are dueling
Revelry and a face full of sorrow
They encounter each other on a
  Venetian street
At the dance in the opera house at
  night
Death appears for the first time
Sporting a silver mask and a black
  overcoat
Nobody knows
If he's the Poet in disguise

Rouge chamber, spiral staircase
A masked naked lady holding her
  breasts, herself on offer
Life's a sumptuous, indulgent feast
How can we not lose ourselves to
  merry-making?

From the plaza to the streets
The three Deaths together stroll
The tall one has a protruding beak

其二罩個金臉
其三是一副骷髏
空洞的下巴
不多的幾顆牙

死神裂嘴
大笑人生的虛妄
卻一無聲響
深巷水聲倒影拍岸

死神抱起裸女
陳屍於黑水
詩人高歌一曲
嘲弄的是自己

教堂裏葬禮隆重而莊嚴
管風琴和彌撒合唱
大理石潔白的雕像前
人們列隊悼念
詩人揭下面具
滿臉的憂傷

哪裏還找得到鮮活的感覺？
又哪裏去找尋心靈的呼應？

The second one sports a golden mask
The third is a skeleton
Their chins are hollow
Their teeth, sparse

The three Deaths are grinning
Laughing at life's futility
But they make no sound
A hidden alley, water's murmur,
Its reflections hit the shore

One Death carries a naked girl
And lays down the corpse in the dark
  water
The Poet sings in a loud voice
Making fun of his own folly

A church, a funeral, solemn,
  ceremonious
The pipe organ plays, people at Mass
  sing in unison
Before a white marble statue
Mourners line up in rows
The Poet takes off his mask
A face full of sorrow is revealed

Where can we find fresh and novel
  feelings?
Where can we find the resonance in
  our hearts?

哪裏再喚得起靈魂的悸動？
而魂魄安在？

一無響應
要知道　現如今
連詞語也喪失了意義
全都成了商品的廣告
你即使呼喚
也只剩個呼叫的姿態
失去魂魄的這你
無非一個虛晃的身影
徒然尋找失落的夢境

一個孤獨的男人
哪裏去找尋
同樣孤寂的女人
在社會的邊緣
一起去承接世界末日？
在世界的終端
重建伊甸園？
另寫一部創世紀？
哪怕僅僅勾畫
純屬內心的一番境界
較之革命和詞語的造反
竟無比艱難！

Where can we awaken the throbbing
  of the soul?
Where is our spiritual being?

There is no response
You must know that, nowadays
Words have lost their meaning
They've all become advertisements for
  goods
Even if you call out
You're left with only the gesture of
  calling
You, who have lost your soul
You're nothing but an empty shadow
  sneaking by
Vainly looking for a lost dream

A lonely man
Where can he find a woman
Who's just as lonely
On the margins of society
To face Doomsday's trials?
To rebuild the Garden of Eden
At the world's end?
Or to write another Book of Genesis?
If only to outline a picture
Of the heart's inner depths?
Compared to a revolution, or to
  words' rebellion
This is much more difficult!

更加虛幻的女人
全然迷失在混沌之中
面孔再變化多端
不過是心中的幻影

只有憂傷才實實在在
牽扯起一個個聯想
如同雲霧中的幻覺
虛無縹緲若隱若現

(4)
窗外雪花飄飄
一個個裸女雕像似乎睡著了
皇家廣場上車輛緩緩而行
當心路滑恰如行人

雪中的公園靜悄悄
雪吸收了一切含義
聽到的只是
默默的心思

為甚麼是倫敦街頭？
全然沒有緣由
只因為飄雪
雄獅也凍僵了

A woman, even more illusory
Vanishes completely into the misty
  mass
No matter how changeful the face
  might be
It's only a phantom in the mind

Only sorrows are real enough
To prompt successive associations
Like mirages in the fog
Chimerical, tenebrous, indistinct

(4)
Snowflakes flutter outside the window
Nude female statues look as if they're
  asleep
In Royal Plaza, the cars are slowly
  moving
Mindful, like the pedestrians, of the
  slippery road

It's quiet in the snow-covered park
The snow has absorbed all meaning
One can only hear
The silence of the mind

Why the streets of London?
For no reason at all
Only because of the flying snow
Even the lions are frozen stiff

火車夜行
雪原在車窗外移動
你一無所有
只剩下惆悵

可你好富裕
這珍貴的情感
世界卻如此貧困
失去了哀傷
惟有利益和權力的較量
歸根到柢不過是牟利
世界弄成現今這樣子
又怎麼能不令人沮喪？

霰雪紛飛
深海浪湧
大西洋黑浪滾滾
一名少女提裙遙望

深秋早寒
一個上年紀的女人
不忍年華就此消逝
雙手掩面

The train chugs along in the night
A snowy plain is moving, outside the
window
You have nothing
Except disconsolation

Nonetheless, you're very rich
You still have this precious feeling
But the world is poor
It has lost its sorrow
It has only the strife between interests
and power
In the end, it cares for nothing but
profit
The world has come to be like this
How can we not feel depressed?

Driving sleet coming down in all
directions
Billowing waves swirling in the deep
blue sea
In the Atlantic, black swells are rolling
A young girl, holding her dress, looks
into the distance

Late Autumn, morning chill
A woman, aging
Cannot bear to see the passage of her
prime
Buries her face in her hands

一座中世紀的死城
陪伴一個黑衣女人
想要述說甚麼
終於甚麼也沒說
不過是詩人的獨白
同黑衣女人的沉默
剪接成一個個句子
如同荒草和廢墟連接

教堂內屍骸橫陳
死亡就這樣嘲弄生命
活生生的性命當其時
何嘗不也戲弄一番死亡？
一名裸女便肆無忌憚
橫臥在風車之下
騷姿弄首於殘垣之前

死神哈哈大笑
而女人哀歌
粉白的斷牆前
垂首轉身
沉浸在歌聲中
情趣自得
看腳尖旋轉

A medieval ghost town
Keeps company with a woman in
black
There's an urge to say something
But nothing's said in the end
Only the Poet's soliloquy
And the silence of the woman in black
They are spliced into sentences
As weeds bind together with ruins

An array of corpses lies in the church
Thus does death make a mockery of
life
When life is full of vivacity
Is it not also toying with death?
Unscrupulously a naked woman
Reclines beneath a windmill
Flaunting her stuff before crumbling
walls

Death laughs aloud
And the woman sings a doleful song
Before a dilapidated, whitewashed
wall
She turns and bows her head
Engrossed in her own singing
Happy and content
She pirouettes as she stares at the tips
of her toes

一個木偶在跳舞
是詩人在耍弄死亡
既然死無法抗拒
乾脆作一場遊戲
和死神一同起舞

女巫率領一群玩偶
一匹馬　頭伸出窗口
一個瘋女人滔滔不絕
獅子在門洞裏吼叫
流浪漢發表演說
說的是世界已無可救藥

街頭賣藝人戴一頂草帽
一副黑眼鏡懸掛在帽沿
牆壁上一顆石頭俯視
玻璃破碎黑洞洞的窗口

大街空蕩蕩
只有幾隻腳倒騰
一座沒有臉面的雕像
一隻手扒住屋檐
一個人吊在街心
一艘郵輪從天邊馳近

A puppet performs a dance
It's the Poet toying with death
Since Death cannot be resisted
Might as well turn life into a game
And dance with Death

A witch leads a troupe of dolls
A horse sticks its head out of the
  window
A mad woman incessantly babbles
A lion roars inside his cave
A tramp delivers a speech
Proclaiming the world to be beyond
  redemption

A busker puts on a straw hat
A pair of sunglasses rests on the brim
On a wall, a stone overlooks
The holes in a shadowy, broken-paned
  window

The main street is empty
Except for a few feet moving about
A faceless statue
A hand clutching at an eave
A man hanging in the middle of the
  street
A cruise ship approaching from the
  horizon

(5)
一戴上面具
人生便如戲
而如戲的人生
真的變成假的
真假混雜
再也弄不清
老演員掀開面具
縱聲大笑
笑這世界何其荒謬

生命出於偶然
美則更為蹊蹺
偶然之中的偶然
就那麼一瞬間
一個眼神
恰巧被另一雙慧眼
發現　捕捉　凝聚　定焦
從而成為影像
誰有幸看到
便銘記在心
詩人的幸運

各種各樣的表情
喜怒哀樂輪流操作
像是做面部的體操

(5)
Once you've put on a mask
Life then becomes a play
And in this theater of life
What's real becomes false
They're all mixed up
No one can tell them apart
An old actor takes off his mask
He bursts out laughing
At the world and how absurd it has
become!

Life comes from an accident
But Beauty is even more intriguing
It's an accident among accidents
For a fleeting moment
A certain look is by chance discovered
Discovered, captured, aimed at, and
focused on
By another pair of eyes of wisdom
It's then converted into an image
The lucky person who sees it
Will keep it forever in his mind
The luck of the poet

All kinds of expressions
Happiness, anger, sorrow, and joy
Put on their act one by one
Just like a performance of facial
gymnastics

人生的千姿百態
總還有點看頭

劇烈的表情
平靜的憂傷
輪流交替
人生百態
如同做戲

偶然一面之緣
如此這般一幅幅場景
隨後是長長的鏡頭
一個個畫面緩慢而平靜
總也在演變
有如幻覺
又如同夢境
卻真真切切
那切膚之痛
其時又恍恍惚惚
感覺的究竟是刀刃
還是皮膚？

不知是不是做白日夢
一個裸女躺在沙發上
身裹透明的輕紗在飛天
一個孩子在空地上張望
而舞女騰空表演柔術
展翼飛翔像是天使

Manifestations of life's kaleidoscope
They are nonetheless worth looking at

Violent emotion
Calm sadness
They alternate and take turns
The myriad scenarios of life
Just like what happens in a play

It's a chance encounter
Scene after scene appears just like that
Followed by very long shots
The frames appear slowly and quietly
  one by one
Changing perpetually
Like hallucinations
Or what happens in a dream
But they're real, material
The pain cuts into one's skin
You're dazed, at the time
Don't know if it's the blade that's
  feeling
Or if it's your skin?

Maybe it's a daydream
A naked woman lies on the sofa
Her translucent veil flutters in the air
A child surveys an open space
A female dancer performs judo while
  in flight
Flying like a winged angel

又像女巫伸展黑袍
俯視亂糟糟的世界
張開雙臂悉盡包裹

一個壞孩子
躲在女人們大腿間
又好奇還又詭譎
那一張盈盈笑臉

(6)
再隨後是雲層
機翼下緩緩移動
從高空俯視
風起而雲湧
浩渺無垠
險像叢生
時而又迷茫如夢
令人止不住遐想
人生倘若果真如雲
豈不也妙趣橫生

雲影下戈壁浩瀚
永恆的寂寞
一無聲響
緩緩移動
遲遲才隱隱傳來
一丁點音樂

Or like a witch in a billowing black
robe
Overlooking the chaotic world
Her arms open, she embraces all

A mischievous child
Hides between a woman's thighs
Curious yet duplicitous
His face beaming with a smile

(6)
Then the clouds follow
They move slowly under the wings of
the plane
Looking down, from high in the sky
They rise up, driven by the wind
In the vast expanse
Scenes of constant danger
Sometimes they're confusing, as in a
dream
Tempting people to indulge in reveries
If life were like the clouds
Wouldn't it be so much fun

Beneath the shadows of the clouds lies
the vast Gobi Desert
Eternal solitude
Sound's total absence
Slowly, it moves
Wafting faintly through the air
A few bars of belated music

啊，遲來的春天柳條依依
寬闊的草場雪山在望
一棵枯殘的老樹等待截肢
一個農婦在門前用裙子擦手
一位老者站住呆望
一個女人呼天搶地
痛哭的不知是
喪失的丈夫還是兒子

哀歌悠遠
一座農舍空蕩蕩
頹敗的閣樓
封閉了的教堂
惟有死者的墓碑在守望

(7)
一個個赤腳的模特兒戴的奶罩
身裹透明的包裝紙
各色各樣的泡沫塑料
有拎鞋子的或揮舞提包

女士們　先生們，
你們瞧！
要一切全都是假的
這世界該多麼美妙！

Oh, Spring arrives late, its willow trees
lingering
A sweeping meadow overlooks a snowy
mountain
A shriveled old tree awaits amputation
In front of the door a peasant woman
Wipes her hands upon her skirt
An old man blankly stands and stares
A woman, with grief, screams bitterly
Nobody knows if she is crying
For the loss of her husband or her son

Songs of lament in the distance
An empty farmhouse
A dilapidated loft
A closed-down church
Only the tombstones of the dead are
keeping watch

(7)
The models are barefoot, bra-clad
Cloaked in transparent wrapping paper
Made of different kinds of plastic and
foam
Some carrying shoes or parading their
purses

Ladies and gentlemen
Please take a look!
If everything were fake
How wonderful the world would be!

沒有藝術
沒有含意
您儘管隨意胡搞
只要能推銷

沒有信仰
沒有記憶
只誇誇其談
還無須思想

也沒有音樂
只有音響
震耳欲聾
要不，戛然打住！

一個豔裝酒吧女兩腿岔開
剛轉身第二個趕緊亮相
更加挑逗還加倍惹眼
第三個跟著上場
赤裸得只剩下三點

生命無非是生命
要甚麼意義？
也沒有希望
希望即虛妄

No art
No hidden meanings
You are free to mess around
As long as what you make can be sold!

No beliefs
No memories
Only big words and hyperboles are left
And no need for thinking

And no music
Only sounds
Ear-splitting noise
That can suddenly cease and stop
altogether!

A garishly-dressed bargirl spreads her
legs
As soon as she turns away, another
hurries out
She's more provocative and more
striking
A third girl follows
Naked except for three vital parts

Life is nothing more than life itself
Why must it be meaningful?
And hope does not exist either
It's no different from delusion

三名吧女躺在圓盤上
旋轉出風情種種
沒有甚麼比這更容易
還樂得輕鬆
新時代就此來臨
歷史從此告終

四個男人西服革履
前後左右把住路口
雙手一律插進口袋
不知是做時裝廣告
還是僱傭來的保鏢

搖滾樂於是四起
此起彼伏一片嚎叫
說是發洩
又像尋熱鬧

一條黑布長長如龍
緩緩移動
順次鑽出四個男人
有戴黑眼鏡的
有的叼根雪茄

The three bar girls lie on a big round
plate
They gyrate and move coquettishly
Nothing is easier than this
Just relax and enjoy yourself
A new age has arrived
History has now come to an end

Four men in suits and ties
Keeping guard, left and right, front
and back
Their hands in their pockets
Don't know if they are filming a
commercial
Or hired bodyguards

And then rock music blasts from all
directions
Howling and growling, with every rise
and fall
Maybe people are venting their spleen
Or just looking for noise and
excitement

A black cloth as long as a dragon
Slowly crawls along
Four men in succession worm their
way out
One wears a pair of shades
The other has a cigar in his mouth

有戴禮帽的
有撐的陽傘

隨後拖出的女人
像剛打撈的溺水女子
一串長長的悲歌
一聲絕望的喊叫
又像風聲在呼嘯

(8)
一名女演員淩空步行
兩手張開雙目閉緊
靠得住的唯有自己
你們説甚麼她一概不信

説人生如夢
還不如説人生如煙
生命猶如懸絲一縷
上一刻還清清楚楚
下一刻便烟消雲散

她也知道這一閃念
不過是個意象
停佇之時
便從中得趣
而實實在在的人生
不知在何處

Another sports a top hat
The last one holds an umbrella in his
hand

Next they drag out a woman
She looks like she's just been saved
from drowning
A long string of sad songs
A cry of despair
Like the wind's howling

(8)
An actress walks in the air
Hands outstretched, eyes closed tightly
She trusts only herself
She doesn't believe you, whatever you
say

They say that life is a dream
It's better to say that life's a puff of
smoke
Or a dangling silken thread
One moment it's clear for all to see
The next, it dissipates and is no more

She also knows that this flashbulb
memory
Is just an image
While it stays on
It gives you pleasure
But life, the life of reality
Is nowhere to be seen

沒有奇蹟
只有約會
也沒有幻想
有的只是床第之間
愛情一個空洞的字眼
不如時裝不斷翻新

(9)
詩人手持詩篇
向同桌十二個男人朗誦
眾人前俯後仰
不亦樂乎
詩人撂下詩篇
不勝惶惑
眾人於是哈哈大笑
詩人憤憤然追問：
是誰把美葬送了？
霎時一片譁然
盤子裏的黑墨潑灑一桌
莊重的晚餐不歡而散

落魄的王子沒有歸宿
曠野裏徘徊困頓不堪
偏偏遇上沮喪的詩人
誰也解救不了誰

No miracles
Only dates
No fantasies either
Only what happens between the sheets
Love is a hollow word
Unlike fashion, which constantly
  renews itself

(9)
The Poet, holding a poem in his hand,
Recites to the twelve men at the table
All are in high spirits
Noisily bending forward and
  backward
The bewildered Poet throws down the
  poem
And becomes terrified in the extreme
Everyone screams and laughs out loud
Angrily, the Poet asks:
Who annihilated Beauty?
Instantly there is an uproar
The black ink in the plate splatters
  over the table
A grand dinner, a solemn occasion,
  breaks up in displeasure

A down-and-out prince has no place
  to call home
Exhausted, he wanders the wilds
He encounters the despondent Poet
Neither can save the other

默默相望
之後如喪家之犬
彼此嗅了嗅
各自轉身走開

湖泊已經乾枯
天鵝都飛走了
只剩下一汪沼澤
王子在泥潭中跪下

唐吉訶德又老又瘦
揮舞一把破傘
可憐的騎士哪裏撐得住
這搖搖欲墜的世界

面對四面來風
新聞八卦層出不窮
哈姆雷特利劍出鞘
竟然找不到敵人
束手無策
四顧茫然

長長的餐桌一張
門徒分坐兩旁
詩人替代了基督
端坐中央當仁不讓
舉手示意要發表演説
不料眾人竟紛紛起鬨
隨即齊聲唱起搖滾

Face to face, they stare in silence
Then, like stray dogs
They sniff each other
Turn, and walk away

The lake has dried up
The swans have flown
Leaving behind only a quagmire
The prince kneels down in the mud

Don Quixote, old and bony
Brandishing a broken umbrella
How could this miserable knight uphold
A world on the verge of collapse?

Rumours spread in all directions
Endless gossip, from the news, pours in
Hamlet draws his sword from its
  scabbard
But he can't find any enemy
He doesn't know what to do
He looks around, confused

A long dining table
The disciples sitting on both sides
The Poet takes the place of Jesus Christ
In the middle of the table he assumes
  his role
Raising his hand to signal a speech
Unexpectedly the disciples kick up a row
Together they sing rock songs

詩人就勢改變手勢
權且充當一回指揮

也還是這張長桌
眾人圍住那主發牌
只見他掀開手中的一張
眾人騰的全都站了起來

上帝其時已變成乞丐
邋裏邋遢蹣跚而來
向眾人一一伸手
甚麼也乞討不到

上帝在天庭震怒了
降災難於人世
末日審判於是來臨
這人世一片混亂
造物主冷眼靜觀
無意拯救

The Poet plays along and changes his
act
And serves as conductor for the time
being

Still at the same long table
A man, surrounded by a crowd, deals
out playing cards
As soon as he turns over the card in
his hand
Everyone jumps and stands on their
feet

At that time, God has turned into a
beggar
Wobblingly He teeters along
And reaches out His hand to the
crowd
But He comes up empty

This incurs the wrath of God in
Heaven
He decrees that disaster should befall
mankind
So the Last Judgement arrives
Pandemonium ensues all over the
world
The Creator watches with indifference
He has no intention of lending a hand

(10)
進此門得一分鐘靜心
出此門得一分鐘凝視

門徑自打開
大廳空蕩蕩
隱隱約約
晃過個人影
誘你前行

一聲聲腳步
一重又一重的門
一個個不分男女
進入地獄之前
過往的一生
止不住回顧流連

死神持杖逡巡
跟隨兩位侍從
舉杖指向誰
誰便倒斃
無上威嚴
無從抵擋
所經之處
無人得以寬恕

詩人同死神照面
死神舉起拐杖

(10)
Enter the door and get one minute of
meditation
Exit the door and get one minute of
gazing

The way to the door is already open
The hall is big, the hall is empty
A shady figure, lurking in the shadows
Beckons you to step inside

Unending footsteps, from one door to
another
People passing by; not clear if they're
men or women
Before they enter Hell
They cannot help but linger
And look back upon their lives now
past

Death walks his beat, staff in hand
Two attendants tag along
When he points his staff at someone
Sudden death will fall on them
His power is supreme
His wish can't be denied
Wherever he goes
None is spared, none forgiven

The Poet meets Death, face to face
When Death raises his staff

詩人再桀驁不馴
不得不雙手蒙面

一女子以淚洗臉
一女子垂下長髮
一男人喊而無聲
一老者雙膝跪下

一個又一個奇怪的姿勢
一聯串怪異的動作
一個個場面莫名其妙
種種行為不明前因後果

不知他或她是誰
偶爾一面之緣
看到一個姿態
聽見一聲叫喊
不明白甚麼含意
事情已經發生
也無須加以解釋
況且也說不清
這無其數的偶然
或稱作命運
或所謂機緣
想要的總也遇不上
從未預料偏偏在眼前

The Poet, though arrogant and unyielding
Can't help but cover his face with his
hands

A woman, her face is awash with tears
Another woman, her long hair is
hanging down
A man, he cries but utters no sound
An old man kneels on both his knees

Uncanny postures, each in turn
Bizarre movements in succession
Scenes bewildering, scenes continual
All things happen without cause or
effect

You didn't know who he or she was
You caught a glimpse of the face at a
casual meeting
Saw a posture
Heard a cry
You didn't understand their meaning
The incident had happened already
There's no need for explanation
Besides, it's inexplicable
Countless accidents
Or so-called chances
Some call them fate
What you desire never comes
The unexpected just happens in front of
your eyes

畫面就這樣剪輯
大千世界可不從來如此
眼看這座地獄之門
浮世繪中芸芸眾生
輾轉反側飽受煎熬
不斷折騰永無止境
總也解不脱的欲望
一幅幅受難的景象

再隨後一組群像
猶如活動的雕塑
一個個人體
煉獄中男男女女
糾纏扭曲
彼此還不斷牽扯
不知是赴死
還是求生？

(11)
基督哪怕是上帝之子
且不説拯救不了世人
甚至無法拯救自己
人世如此混濁
還有甚麼值得信仰？
又哪裏找尋崇高的精神？

That's how the scenes have been set
But the world is never like that
Look at what happens at the gate of
  Hell
All the living creatures depicted in
  ukiyo-e
They're tossing and turning, they're
  being tortured
Endless pain, interminable agonies
Scene after scene of people suffering
Who can't extricate themselves from
  desire

Then comes a group picture
Just like a statue that moves
This huge mass of bodies
Men and women in purgatory
Entangled and twisted
They pull and clutch at one another
Not clear if they're facing death
Or if they're seeking life?

(11)
Even though Jesus was God's son
Not only did He fail to save the people
He also could not save Himself
The world is filthy
What else is left that's worth believing?
Where could we find any noble spirit?

上帝既然已經死了
上帝之子耶穌基督
且已死在這之前
剩下一個又一個
自稱為救世的主
世界由他們糟搞
可不是越搞越糟

連記憶全都抹去
只剩下一片虛無
既然歷史已經終結
剩下的不過是塗鴉
既然意義也已喪失
又何必再去書寫？

既然人們宣告
上帝從此已死
索性無所事事
與其像個叫化子
甚麼也乞討不到
不如做個流浪漢
在人欲橫流的世上
縱觀行人匆匆過往

這是一個沒有救贖的時代
有的只是各種各樣的商標
這是一個無比偉大的時代

Since God is already dead
And Jesus Christ, the Son of God
Died before Him
We're left with self-proclaimed saviors
Appearing one after another
If we let them make a mess of the
  world
It'll only become messier and messier

Even memories have all been erased
Leaving only a vast and voided swathe
Since History has already ended
The rest is only graffiti
Since meaning has been lost
Why do we still bother to write?

People have already declared
That God is dead
He might as well idle His time away
If He becomes a beggar
And gets nothing in the end
Why not make Himself a tramp
In this world infested with desires
And watch pedestrians hurry by?

This is the age which has no
  redemption
Except all kinds of trademarks
This is the age of unequaled
  grandiosity

大樓一座比一座蓋的更高
精神一個比一個更矮小

上帝造人時何曾想到
造出的人類無比貪婪
這般狡猾還如此狂妄
又怎麼能不沮喪？
唯獨撒旦暗中竊笑
向死神一再擠眉弄眼

歌星於是縱情高唱：
這世界如此美妙
啊，如此美妙
美妙得沒治了！

唯獨一位老者
步履蹣跚
遍地徒然找尋
喪失了的憐憫之心

午夜的廣場空寂
思想者從石座上下來
同迎面而來的詩人相望
久久凝視而默默無言

Huge buildings built taller and taller
But the human spirit gets smaller and
 smaller

When God made men
How could He have known that they
 could be so greedy
So cunning and so unscrupulous
How could He not be depressed?
Only Satan snickers in secret
Winking at Death again and again

The famous singer thus sings with
 abandon:
What a wonderful world
Oh yes, so wonderful
So wonderful that it is beyond cure!

A lonely old man
Unsteady, walking awkwardly
He looks everywhere in vain
For the heart of mercy that's been lost

At midnight, the plaza is deserted
The Thinker gets up from his stone
 seat
He and the oncoming Poet look at
 each other
For a long time, they stare in silence

(12)
人群迷失在摩天樓群中
車輛穿行於燈光之間
永遠忙忙碌碌
不知何處是歸屬

人們紛紛詢問：
究竟何去何從？
卻無人知道
這問也徒勞

而人群簇簇
還前推後擁
世界總也亂糟糟
一人呼叫
便嚷成一片
究竟喊甚麼？
誰也聽不清
有人伸手
眾人都去搆
到底要甚麼？
只有天知道
到頭來
甚麼也抓不到

背後那隱形的黑手
只能感覺蛛絲馬跡
等你轉身了無蹤影
卻總也在周遭算計

(12)
The crowd is drifting among
skyscrapers
Cars are busy shuttling between lights
People hustling, bustling all the time
They don't know where they belong

People are asking one after another:
Where are we really going?
No one knows the answer
Asking is futile

A large crowd has gathered
They push and shove each other
The world is in constant disorder
When one man shouts
Others will shout with him
What are they shouting?
No one can hear clearly
When someone stretches out his hand
Everybody wants to reach for it
What do they really want?
Heaven only knows
In the end, they all come up
empty-handed

The invisible black hand hiding behind
You can only feel its presence
It will vanish when you turn your back
But it's still there, still plotting, still
scheming

人肉炸彈隨時可能拉響
摩天樓再高霎時崩塌
恰如紙牌疊起的股市
風吹草動便搖搖欲墜

天天聽的是政客們
此起彼伏競選的謊言
六根一刻不得清靜
媒體垃圾鋪天蓋地
又如何清理得乾淨？

真理弄成招搖過市的一塊破布
正義也蛻變成揮之不去的病毒
叫所有人一概過敏
喪失嗅覺只打噴嚏

現如今通行的
只有一個字眼：
錢！
印製鈔票比手紙還快
成噸成噸以億萬計
撒向全世界

A human bomb can explode any
minute
Skyscrapers, however tall, can collapse
in an instant
The stock market is like a house of
cards
Just a small breeze will make it fall

We must listen, every day, to
politicians
And their interminable campaign lies
Our ears don't have a moment's peace
Trashy media envelop the world
How can all of this be cleansed?

Truth has been made into a rag,
swaggering through the street
Righteousness has been turned into a
virus which will not go away
All this has driven people to become
allergic
They can only sneeze, having lost their
sense of smell

Nowadays there's only one word that
is ubiquitous:
Money!
Money's printed faster than toilet
paper
Ton after ton, in billions and trillions
Being thrown at the world entire

與其由媒體天天侃侃而談
你何嘗不也面對世界發言
一個人直面人生說自己的話
中不中聽不在話下
況且說就說了
也就了然釋然
並非為後代留言
端起架子當聖賢
而聖人都早已安息
世界卻不見太平

更何況上帝已死
其子基督也白白犧牲
只見一個又一個超人
世界由他們重新打造
怎麼能不越弄越糟糕

地下管道錯綜複雜
嘶嘶聲響令神經緊張
剎那間如瓦斯爆炸
一個個目瞪口呆
身體緊貼住烏黑的牆皮

Instead of the media's hot air each day
Why don't you speak directly to the
world?
Face life head on, all by yourself
Say the words from your heart
Whether people like it or not
That's their problem
Besides, once the words are said, that's
them done with
You'll feel relieved, at ease
It's not for the sake of posterity
Or putting on the air of saints or sages
Long have they been resting in peace
Yet the world is far from being peaceful

Moreover, God is already dead
And His Son Jesus was sacrificed in vain
Supermen appear, one after another
If they were to re-create the world
Wouldn't they just make it worse?

Intricate piping in the underpass
Emits a nerve-wracking hiss
Suddenly there's something like a gas
explosion
Everyone gasps, stunned and
speechless
Their bodies closely huddling against
the blackened wall

無可後退猶如絕境
這場景就像集體屠殺
一群赤裸的人體
塞在關閉的電梯裏
如同囚籠
恐懼與絕望
令汗血一概冰冷

(13)
歷史總也不斷重複
人們恰如熱鍋上的螞蟻
依然成日價急急匆匆
並不知道究竟去哪裏
這才是人類最深刻的悲劇
誠然又是一齣絕妙的喜劇
而悲喜交加　荒誕加怪誕
人生如戲　可不如此這般

問題恐怕只在於
觀眾的位置在哪裏？
這多少才算個真問題
徒有演員而無觀眾

In a blind alley, they have nowhere to go
The scene is like a massacre
A group of naked people
Trapped in a lift with its doors tightly
shut
A cage full of prisoners
Despair and fear
Have turned all their blood and sweat
As cold as ice

(13)
History never fails to repeat itself
People act like ants in a pan
Scurrying here and there all day
Having no idea where it is they are
headed
This is mankind's most profound
tragedy
Surely it's also a wonderful comedy
Sorrow and happiness are blended
together
As are the absurd and the grotesque
They say that life is like a play
But it's certainly not like that

There is only one problem:
Where are the seats for the audience?
This is more or less where the real
problem lies:
There are actors but no audience

戲演得哪怕再精彩
無人觀賞有何意義？

問題進而又在於
看到的都是包裝好的節目
而生菜也苦
都打了農藥
牛排豬排全注入激素
到海水也深深污染
魚無須打撈全漂浮水面
這世界才真叫美妙
只剩下無所不能的人
無比貪婪
無止境消費
加速度瘋狂
止都止不住
不知道何謂滿足

直到有一天
能源耗盡
林木全剃得精光
無聲無息還無風
連地球也拒絕旋轉

No matter how wonderful the
performance
What's the use if there's nobody to see it?

There are also other problems:
All the shows we see have been
pre-packaged
The lettuces have become bitter
Sprayed with pesticide and chemicals
Steaks and pork chops, injected with
hormones
Even seawater is heavily polluted
Fish, never caught, all float to the
surface
This all really makes for a really
wonderful world
Only people capable of doing anything
are left
Infinite greed
Endless consumption
Senseless acceleration
There's no stopping them
They're insatiable

Then the day will come
With all resources depleted
And the trees and forests shaved to the
ground
Windless silence
When even the Earth shall refuse to
rotate

去烏有之鄉之前
姑且停一分鐘
　靜默！
屏住呼吸
觀審和傾聽
此時此刻
所作所為
是否必要？

且慢一拍！
不為人先
看一看前人的腳印
再看看樹葉飄逸
隨後聽風聲沉吟
重新領悟生命的含意
回顧身後這路如何再走？
又是否值得？

就這樣到了一個街口
每天經過竟忽略了
街角一抹斜陽
陽臺上牽個風箏
恰如兒時的希望
而明朝是否看得到藍天？

你於是聽見腳步下
這長長的身影

Before going to Utopia
Let's stop for one minute of silence!
Hold our breath, observe, and listen
At this moment, whatever we're doing
Is it really all that necessary?

Slow down!
Don't strive to be the first
Take a look at our predecessors'
  footprints
Admire the natural grace of the leaves
Listen to the murmur of the wind
Once again, apprehend the hidden
  meaning of life
Look back and contemplate how to
  tread the path of your future
Will it be worth your while?

You've come to a street junction
You pass this place every day
But you've been ignoring
The setting sun's touch on the corner
  of the street
The kite hanging from the balcony
Just like what you longed, as a child,
  to see
But will you be able to see the blue sky
  tomorrow?

Then you hear footsteps
An elongated shadow

竟然勾起另一個
久已喪失的印象
銀鈴般的歌喉婉轉
令心頭一熱
止不住老淚橫流
如今早已人逝物非
何從撿回散失的記憶？

(14)
匆匆過往的行人
恰如一行行螞蟻
而生命瞬間即逝
不死於車禍
便死於戰爭
暗中一顆槍子
迎面一聲爆炸
還來不及叫喊
已魂消魄散
至於不治之症
好歹苟延殘喘
不能不算幸運
而焦慮和頹喪
可是不治之症
喪失掉記憶
死亡的前兆

For no reason evokes
Another long lost impression
Mellow singing, just like silver bells' chimes
It warms the heart
You can't stop your tears from falling
From your weathered eyes
Now things have changed and people passed away
How will you retrieve the lost memories?

(14)
Pedestrians scurry by
Like row on row of ants
Life is fleeting, it's gone in a flash
If people don't die in car accidents
They'll die in a war
A bullet from a hidden gun
An explosion in your face
Before you've had the time to scream
You've melted away and dissolved
And then there are terminal diseases
Even if you manage to prolong your ailing existence
You cannot say that you are not lucky
Anxiety and depression
They're incurable
The loss of your memories
A forewarning of death

這才想起生活該有的品質
過一天混一天也算是人生？
何時才能重見黎明的徵兆？
又如何領悟生命的含義？

告訴我們！
告訴我們！
告訴我們！
怎樣才能得到寬恕？
怎樣才能得以解救？
怎樣才能重見美的曙光？
維納斯動人心弦那嬌美的形象？

一家家閃過的店面和櫥窗
一個接一個長長的隧道

一群男人簇擁
一名赤身垂危的女子
抬起手腳　扛在肩上
氣喘吁吁　奔跑不息

Only then are we reminded of the
quality of life
How can life be life if we only muddle
through it?
When can we again see the sign of
dawn breaking?
How do we apprehend the hidden
meaning of life?

Tell us!
Tell us!
Tell us!
How can we be forgiven?
How can we be saved?
How can we again see Beauty's
aurora?
Venus's lovely, heart-stirring image?

One by one, speed past store fronts
and windows
In succession, the long, extended
tunnels

A group of men forms a circle
Around a naked, dying woman
They lift her hands and feet and carry
her on their shoulders
Panting and gasping, they keep on
running

不知是擄掠還是拯救
女人們捂面哭泣不已

高速公路永遠是同樣的路標
車窗外閃閃而過的樓群和廣告

維納斯無聲無息
躺在圍觀的眾人腳下
喃喃吶吶議論聲中
一灘黑水在腿下流淌
男的低頭女的捂面
一個個散去不忍再看

死了？
死了？
死了！

沒有回應
沒有聲響
沒有動靜
沒有氣息

眾聲疊起
死了，死了，死了……
就這樣

Ignorant whether they're ravaging or
  rescuing
The other women cover their faces, cry
  uncontrollably

Highways sport the same signs
Outside the car window, buildings and
  billboards flash by

Venus is dying, at her last breath
Lying at the feet of surrounding
  onlookers
Amidst whispers and arguments
A black water pool flows beneath her legs
The men lower their heads, the women
  cover their faces
Disperse, one by one, unable to look on

Dead?
Dead?
Dead!

No response
No sound
No motion
No breathing

Many people speaking, one after
  another
Dead, dead, dead...
Just like that

扼殺了
窒息了
踐踏了
犧牲了
葬送了
了結了

(2011 年 11 月 24日)

Strangled
Suffocated
Trampled
Sacrificed
Annihilated
Finished

(24th November 2011)

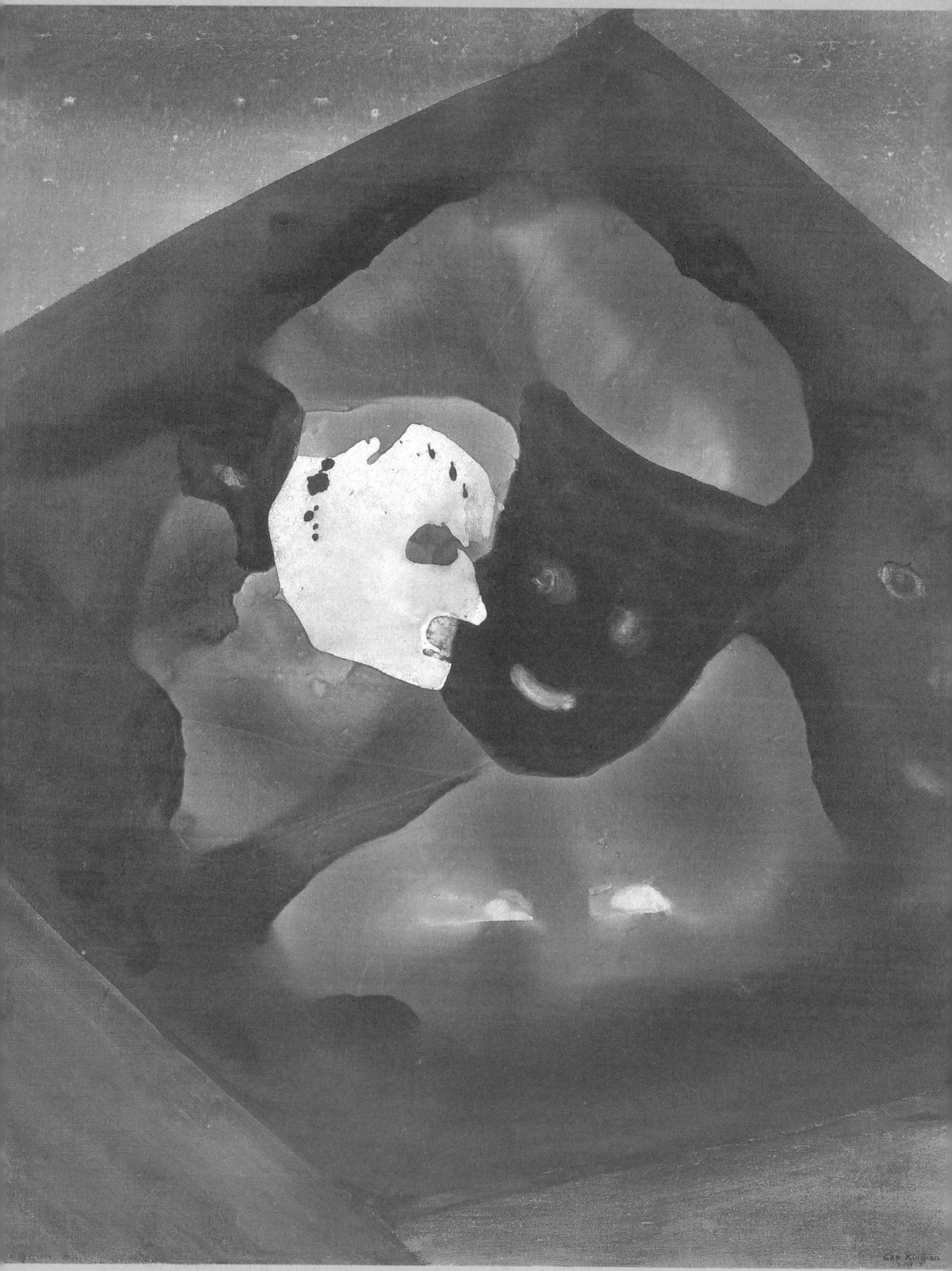

短詩輯錄
Short Poems

《眾生相》*Multiple Illusions*
2011, 100cm × 81cm.

《裏裏外外》
Interior and Exterior
1991,
81.5cm × 96cm.

打開甚麼

打開門
　一陣風聲
打開窗戶
　一隻死鳥
打開自己
　喃喃囈語
關上門
　看不見海
關上窗戶
　剩下燈光
關了燈
　面對黑暗
你
又不是你
　又不是我
走進隧道
　一頂禮帽
　　　掀開禮帽
　一隻蝴蝶
　　　　　折斷翅膀
掀開翅膀
　一隻懷錶
打開錶
　　一隻甲蟲
打開甲蟲
　一窩螞蟻
捅開螞蟻窩
　　　全爬了出來

Open What

Open the door
 The sound of the wind
Open the window
 A dead bird
Open your self
 Muttering and murmuring
Close the door
 Can't see the sea
Close the window
 Only the light is left
Turn off the light
 Face the darkness
You
You are not you
 You are not me
Enter the tunnel
 A top hat
 Take off the top hat
 A butterfly
 Broken wings
Spread the wings
 A pocket watch
 Open the watch
 A beetle
Open the beetle
 A nest of ants
Poke open the nest
 They all crawl out

打開石榴
　　紅的
打開信箱
　　空的
打不開牢籠
　　打得開鎖
撐開雨傘
再打開
處女的禁忌
唯獨
揭不開
　　　那一臉虛偽
打開龍頭
　　嘩嘩流淌
打開字典
　　滿滿一篇
打開
不該打開的
　白睜一雙大眼

Open the pomegranate
 Red
Open the mailbox
 Empty
Can't open a cage
 Can open a lock
Open an umbrella
Then break down
The virgin's taboo
Only
Fail to break open
  The face of hypocrisy
Turn on the tap
 Splashing and sloshing water
Open the dictionary
 Pages full of words
Open
That which shouldn't be opened
 Open a pair of big eyes in vain

誰怕張三

誰怕維吉妮亞·吳爾芙？
恰如誰怕張三
誰怕誰都不怕
張三是隻狼？
維吉妮亞是一頭母虎？
怕與不怕都只是一句話

反抗語言
恰如反抗影子
反抗影子
恰如語言的反抗
反抗反抗
恰如陷阱
誰落進去誰都不幸

Who's Afraid of John Doe?

Who's afraid of Virginia Woolf?
Just like who's afraid of John Doe
Who's afraid and who's not afraid
Is John Doe a wolf?
And Virginia a tigress?
Whoever's afraid or unafraid, they're
merely words

To resist language
It's just like resisting a shadow
To resist a shadow
It's just like the resistance of language
Resist, resist
It's just like a trap
Whoever falls in is unlucky

悼梅新

酒醇茶未涼
詩還在
一位朋友
猝然走了

默默端坐
聽風聲雨聲
等子夜電話
造化如常

鏡泊湖畔
或北市酒吧
再一同杯中撈月
玉山雪總也不化

Mourning Mei Xin

The wine is mellow, the tea not yet
  cold
The poem still lingers
A friend
He is suddenly gone

Wordless, peacefully sitting
To the wind and rain, listening
Waiting for a midnight phone call
The world is its usual self

On Mirror Lake's shore
Or in a bar in North City
Let's drink one more cup to catch the
  moon in the water
The snow on Jade Mountain never
  melts

吐棄

說甚麼？
牙掉了
不用嚼碎
吐棄
比做甚麼
都來得容易

Spit It Out

What are you saying?
The teeth have fallen out
Don't bother chewing it up
Spit it out
Nothing is
Easier

鳥語

聽一種不懂的語言
如同聽鳥叫
一群人嘰嘰喳喳
有說還有笑
恰如一群鳥

鳥兒一來一窩蜂
瞧！那人
好一本正經！
沒準在思考？
一個知識分子？
又一個救世主？
啊，真理的化身！
別同他沾邊！

鳥兒一陣風
統統飛走了
淩空轉一圈
落到另一棵樹梢
依然嘰嘰喳喳
沒完沒了
全然沒煩惱

Birds Twitter

Listening to a language that you don't
understand
It's like hearing birds twitter
A group of nattering, chattering people
Sometimes talking, sometimes laughing
Just like a flock of birds

When birds come, they're like a swarm
of bees
Look! Look at that man!
He is so prim and so proper!
Perhaps he is thinking?
An intellectual?
Or another savior?
O, truth personified!
Avoid him like the plague!

Like a gust of wind
The birds all fly away
They turn in a circle, high up in the sky
Then land atop another tree
Still twittering noisily
They never stop
No worries whatsoever

京都有感

入夜醉京都
這花街柳巷
大紅的燈籠
車如流水
馬如龍
發一通狂言
好一個夢
來一首和歌
再一聲清唱
另一種純粹
又一番玄想

Kyoto Thoughts

Drunk at night in Kyoto
In the streets and alleys of ill-repute
With big red lanterns adorned
The hustling and bustling
Of cars and of people
Utter some mad ravings
Dream a happy dream
Chant a *waka*
Then sing a capella
Another kind of purity
Another fantasy

夢的啟示

夢中頓然領悟
你並不屬於這世界
夢中的那你
也為他人不容
只有將自我懸置
才得以自在
你於是隱形優遊
穿梭於人世
或停佇觀望
這眾生的景象
熙熙攘攘變化多端
情趣所至而興致盈然
方才領會
何謂自由
人間世事
頓時清澄

Enlightenment in a Dream

It suddenly dawned on me in a dream
You don't belong to this world
The you, in the dream
You're also not accepted by others
Only when you suspend yourself
Can you be free and easy
So you become invisible, wander around
In the places where humans dwell
Or you stop and observe
All beings' phenomena
The hustle and bustle that keeps on changing
You're intrigued, full of curiosity and zest
Only then can you understand
The true meaning of freedom
All the happenings in the world
At once become crystal clear

夢中

夢中回到童年
故鄉是一座空城
你佇立街心
陽光燦爛
清寂無人
一頂頂草帽
扣住一個個木樁
一動不動
令你悚然
不禁想起兒時夥伴
門口石階長滿苔蘚
親人可不早已作古
你四顧茫然
不如拍張照片
好歹留個紀念
轉身去取相機
竟已出了夢境

In a Dream

In a dream you go back to your
 childhood
Your hometown is an empty city
You stand for a long time in the
 middle of the street
The sun is shining bright
All is quiet, no people about
Except for the many straw hats
Fastened to rows of wooden poles
They are motionless
And this frightens you
You can't help thinking of your child-
 hood friends
And the moss-covered stepping stones
 at the door
Your family and relatives have all
 passed away
You look around, not knowing what
 to do
Maybe you should take a picture
Good or bad, you'll have something
 by which to remember
You turn to get your camera
Suddenly, you're already out of the
 dream

舞蹈

做無緣無故
不可名狀之事
沒頭沒腦
莫名其妙奔跑
抓頭髮起飛
抱住腳直跳
起伏衝撞
都毫無必要
還做得認真
跳得起勁
竭盡心力
做得盡興
供奉一身
卻難以謀生
此乃謂之
舞蹈
原本出於
性情

Dance

Without rhyme or reason
They do things that defy description
Mindlessly, unthinkingly
They run around with no explanation
They grab their hair and soar in the air
They clasp their feet and jump up high
They bounce up and down and end up
  colliding
All totally unnecessary
But with the utmost care
They dance with boundless verve
With all their energy and strength
To their heart's content
Completely offering themselves
But they can't make a living
This, the so-called
Dance
It originates from
Human nature

政治

丟一個線團
讓猫咪去玩
給一個球
叫孩兒們去搶
造一點機會
由人去鑽營
弄一些是非
讓大家辯論
把正義
時時掛在嘴邊
發動戰爭
如同政變
都黑箱操作
容不得公眾討論
是為
政治

Politics

Throw a reel of string
Let the kittens play with it
Toss a ball
Tell the kids to scramble for it
Create a bit of opportunity
Let people jostle for gain
Spread some gossip
Let everybody argue
Talk justice
Always keep it on your lips
Start a war
Just like a coup d'état
All are black box operations
Permitting no public discussion
Such is
Politics

思想

思想
　在火中燃燒
在水中沉靜
　在雲中飄逸
在心中諦聽

Thoughts

Thoughts
   Burn in fire
Become silent in water
   Float elegantly in the clouds
And listen intently in the heart

《舞者》 *The Dancer*
2010, 58.8cm × 55.6cm.

佳句偶拾

(1)
禪思
靜慮
妙有
坐忘

(2)
鎌倉大佛
好生自在

不牽不掛
方為瀟灑

無可無不可
是為透徹

一派虛空
又見清風

(3)
夜雨淅瀝
寂中透靜
翻然覺醒
尚未黎明

(4)
日以繼夜
花開花謝
春去冬來

Occasional Good Lines

(1)
Zen contemplation
Stillness of mind
Presence of absence
Without thought

(2)
The Great Buddha of Kamakura
Complete freedom

Without attachment
Only then can one be at ease

Yes or no, anything goes
That's limpidity

Nothing but sheer emptiness
A clear wind breezes by

(3)
Pattering night rain
Quiet seeps through silence
Suddenly woken from sleep
Still not yet dawn

(4)
Day and night, night and day
Flowers bloom and wither
Spring goes, Winter comes

歲月如斯
恍若流水
人獨憔悴

(5)
斯人已逝
何來足迹？

(6)
伊人在彼岸
相思在此時

(7)
東或者西
概無道理

不明不白
一塌糊塗

不上不下
又非懸置

一團混亂
甚麼都不是

輾轉反側
怎麼都不適

Days and months are the same
Just like flowing water
Man alone is dejected

(5)
My friend has passed away
Where do you find the footprints?

(6)
My friend is on the other shore
Now is the time for mutual thoughts

(7)
East or West
Absolutely no reason

Confused and confounded
Everything's muddled

Neither up nor down
And not suspended either

A big mass of chaos
It's not anything

Tossing and turning
Can't get no comfort

(8)
三月還冷
鳥鳴花不開
好沒心思

(9)
身影偶合
能不叫哥哥？

(10)
其中有
豁然燦然

(11)
四方土地
一方天井
修竹斜影
神閑氣定

(12)
無中生有
盡在其中

(13)
念天地玄黃
看造化無常

(8)
Still cold in March
Birds are singing, but the flowers
  aren't in bloom
Depressed and despondent

(9)
By chance, body and shadow become
  one
Can you not call me brother?

(10)
In this
There's clarity and lucidity

(11)
Land on four sides
Courtyard on one
Slender bamboos, slanting shadows
Leisurely and calm

(12)
Something comes from nothing
It's all in there

(13)
Think: The sky is black, the earth is
  yellow
Look: Fate is fickle

(14)
妙語偶拾
造句把玩

(15)
是是非非人間事
可不是從來如此

(16)
醍醐灌頂
一夜的糊塗
起來近中午
方才醒悟

(17)
望不斷天涯路
回不去時
方為歸屬

(18)
你又見到了
那一抹微笑
在心中刻下
永久的刀痕

(19)
方圓
尺寸
裁剪
領袖

(14)
On occasion, I pick up witty phrases
I make up words and play with them

(15)
Gossip and squabbles in the world of men
Isn't it always so?

(16)
My head is filled with illumination
After one night's muddling
When I got up, it was nearly noon
Only then was I awakened

(17)
Can't see the end of the road to the world's edge
Unable to turn back
Only then is it time to have a sense of belonging

(18)
You see it again
The flash of a smile
In your heart it cuts
A permanent scar

(19)
Circle and square
Foot and inch
To tailor-make
A leader

(20)
一團疑竇
問個通透

(21)
上下求索
人生苦短

(22)
隨意如水
恣意汪洋

(23)
或平靜
或滿盈
蓋不上心
此乃大幸

(24)
一派虛無乃事物本相
只能拾點生活的碎片

(20)
A shadow of doubt
Get to the bottom of it

(21)
Keep searching up and down
Too bad that life is short

(22)
Leisurely like water
Free like the ocean

(23)
Maybe it's peaceful
Maybe it's full
None of that is my concern
That's my good fortune

(24)
Utter emptiness is the true nature of
all things
One can only pick up a few fragments
of living

《哀傷》 *Sadness*
2008, 120cm × 120cm.